BREATHING FIRE

breathing FiRE

CANADA'S NEW POETS

edited by

LORNA CROZIER & PATRICK LANE

Harbour Publishing

Published by
Harbour Publishing
P.O. Box 219
Madeira Park, BC V0N 2H0
Canada

Published with the assistance of the Canada Council and the Government of British Columbia, Cultural Services Branch.

Cover painting and design by Ande Axelrod
Page design and composition by Vancouver Desktop Publishing Centre
Printed and bound in Canada

"Manitou Poem" excerpt from *Afterworlds*, by Gwendolyn MacEwen. Used by permission of the Canadian Publishers, McClelland & Stewart, Toronto.

Canadian Cataloguing in Publication Data

Main entry under title:
  Breathing fire

  ISBN 1-55017-125-9

1. Canadian poetry (English)—20th century.*
I. Crozier, Lorna, 1948– II. Lane, Patrick, 1939–
PS8293.B73 1995   C811'.5408   C95-910772-X   PR9195.7.B73 1995

For Al Purdy: "*the ivory thought/is still warm*"

As in puberty I dreamed my lifelong protector, who showed me
How to navigate impossible rivers, who made me as the world's
       first person, breathing
Fire and poetry
. . . .

And I am become the powerful dreamer who dreams his way through
To reality, to enter and ignite the stone, to illumine
       from within
Its perfect paradox, its name.
— FROM "MANITOU POEM," BY GWENDOLYN MACEWEN

Contents

AL PURDY
Foreword / xv

LORNA CROZIER and PATRICK LANE
Breathing Fire and Poetry / xvi

MARISA ALPS
Calligraphy Lessons / 1
Dancing I / 2
Dancing II / 3
Dreams / 4
Spring Falls / 5

STEPHANIE BOLSTER
Come to the edge of the barn / 7
Many Have Written Poems about Blackberries / 8
Whose Eyes / 9
Alice's Dreamed Garden Contained in a Vase / 10
Transformations / 11

LESLEY-ANNE BOURNE
Think of Him / 12
Cars and Fast–Food / 13
Risks / 14
Night Before / 16
My Mother Turns Fifty / 17
In the Past / 18

THEA BOWERING
Conjuration. / 19
Women in the duty free. / 20
kitchen familiarities: / 21
lost in the transaction: / 23

TIM BOWLING

The Last Sockeye / 25

Young Eagle on a Piling / 27

Tides (A Poem to Myself) / 28

Snowy Owl After Midnight / 30

SIOUX BROWNING

The Perfect Ten / 32

Dark / 33

Striking Camp / 34

SUZANNE BUFFAM

drive thru / 36

Half-light / 37

Homing / 38

Astronomical Love / 39

At Least / 40

anticipating rain / 41

ALISON CALDER

Imagine a picture / 43

Tie me to the place / 44

Lately she can't stand / 45

Sometimes she / 46

October, seeing / 47

MARK COCHRANE

Medea / 48

Latent / 49

Reunion / 51

Mapplethorpe / 53

KAREN CONNELLY
The Word Is Absurd / 54
The Ugly Mermaid / 55
She Returns To The Farm / 57
Family Reunions / 58
From My Father's Hand / 59
Singing / 60
Love has nothing to do with closing your eyes / 61
Ephemeroptera / 62

MICHAEL CRUMMEY
Morning Labrador Coast / 65
Cod (l) / 66
Cigarettes (1) / 67
Apprenticeships / 69
Rivers/Roads / 70
The Road Home / 71
Lilacs / 72

CARLA FUNK
Brother and Sister / 74
Lot's Daughter / 75
Ode To Soap / 76
Baby Stories / 77
He Watches my Wife Nursing; He Avoided my Mouth / 79
Solomon's Wives, No. 144: Fear of horses / 80
Praise for the Zebra / 81

SUSAN GOYETTE
I Know Women / 83
Sisters / 84
Florence / 85

JOELLE HANN
To Speak / 86
No Cure / 87
Black Shirts Drying /88

SALLY ITO
On Translating the Works of Akiko Yosano / 89
Portrait of Snow Country / 90
Sansei / 91
Jews in Old China / 92
Night in Prospector's Valley / 93
Frogs in the Rain Barrel / 94

JOY KIRSTIN
Grandma in June / 95
After the Pacemaker / 96
Summer's Kitchen / 97

TONJA GUNVALDSEN KLAASSEN
My sister's moon through my window / 99
Eclipse / 100
The echo / 101
Ice Man / 102
Fall River / 103
Manitou-night / 104
Mama / 104

BARBARA KLAR
The Home / 106
Meadowing / 107
Former Sestina For Birds And A Girl / 109
Planter's Prayer / 110

EVELYN LAU
Nineteen / 112
Green / 113
Eight Months Later: His House / 115
Where Did You Learn / 115
Father / 116
The Monks' Song / 117
Adult Entertainment / 118
Waking in Toronto / 119

MICHAEL LONDRY
All Canadians Have Wind-Brazen Faces / 120
Lines for Fortune Cookies / 121
Ars Poetica / 122

JUDY MACINNES JR.
Something Round / 124
Surrey Poem / 124
Pumpfish / 125

HEATHER MACLEOD
Touch the Buffalo / 127
Strawberry / 129
Reflection / 131

BARBARA NICKEL
Twin Sisters to be Presented to Society / 132
Marion, 1936: To my Twin Sister / 133
Marion, 1939: To my Twin Sister / 133
Gladys, 1940: To my Twin Sister / 134

KEVIN PAUL
Ceremony / 135
A Pheasant on Deer Mountain / 136
Belly Button / 137
A Fish on Pandora Street / 138
Still Falling / 139

MICHAEL REDHILL
The Return / 141
Deck Building / 142
Phases / 143
Happy Hour / 144
Indian summer / 145
Reconciliation / 146

JAY RUZESKY
Sergei Krikalev on the Space Station Mir / 148
Night of the Skagit County Parade / 150
Crocuses / 151
Single Mother's Garage Sale / 152
Roller Coaster / 154

GREGORY SCOFIELD
Call Me Brother / 157
Talking Because I Have To / 158
That Squawman Went Free / 158
Wrong Image / 159
Kohkum's Lullaby / 161

NADINE SHELLY

A Preoccupation With Bridges / 162

Because my breast is where the fairest doves rest / 163

The Sun Has Bones / 164

ravenous/ 165

Waiting in the River Valley / 166

Long Beach / 166

KAREN SOLIE

Staying Awake / 168

Toad / 170

Dry Mother / 171

CARMINE STARNINO

Picking the Last Tomatoes with my Uncle / 172

The True Story of my Father / 172

Caserta, Italy — 1945 / 173

The Inheritance / 175

SHANNON STEWART

For a Bouquet / 177

My Mother and Asparagus / 178

Books / 179

Renovations / 182

Architecture / 184

Circle Jerk / 184

Acknowledgements / 186

Credits / 187

Foreword

What a peculiar thing it is to see and feel—fifty years later than your own—another generation coming into its strength. And what a privilege.

I think these are excellent poems, much better than the work of my own earlier generation. And the authors do not seem to have experienced the long apprenticeship which I laboured through. They are here by an act of magic, ripened and full blown, youthful but experienced, a gift we have given ourselves.

A poem by Michael Redhill ends: "And in our blanket, our bodies/hold the shape of the people/whose cells we slept in for generations." This new book also seems to me like a gift from those secret others, asleep in our bones—suddenly awaking with these marvellous poems.

— AL PURDY

Breathing Fire and Poetry

During the sixties in Canada, a whole new generation of poets came of age. Born within a few years of one another, Margaret Atwood, John Newlove, Dennis Lee and Gwendolyn MacEwen, to name a few, began giving readings, starting small presses, and publishing in little magazines and books. Following an impressive continuum of talent begun with writers such as Purdy, Page, Birney, Layton and Webb in the previous generation, the quality of their work was cited as evidence that Canadian writing was enjoying an Elizabethan kind of flowering.

The late seventies saw a further blossoming of names appearing regularly in literary magazines: poets such as Bronwen Wallace, Mary di Michele, Dale Zieroth, Roo Borson and Patrick Friesen. They, too, were born within a few years of one another in the late forties or early fifties.

Now there's a whole new group whose poems are beginning to appear in print, poets born between the mid-sixties and the mid-seventies. We have met many of them across Canada in summer writing workshops, and in libraries and universities through our work as teachers and writers-in-residence. Both of us were impressed not only with their poetic skills but also with their passion for poetry, their desire "to illumine from within." We thought it was time someone brought them together between the covers of one book as proof Canada's Elizabethan period continues.

Al Purdy did the same thing we are doing now with two anthologies called *Storm Warning* 1 and *Storm Warning* 2, published in 1971 and 1976. In the early eighties, Dennis Lee edited an anthology called *The New Canadian Poets*. To define "new," he chose poets whose first books had appeared post-1970. As a result, the forty poets in the anthology range from their late twenties (Erin Mouré) to their early sixties (Anne Szumigalski). Although Lee's anthology is a rich compendium of poets, it doesn't focus on one particular generation, something we chose to do because we were interested in the similarities and differences we might find.

After we came up with the concept of the anthology, we approached Harbour Publishing, who generously agreed to take on the project, and called for submissions from across the country. From the hundreds we received, we ended up with fifty we wanted to include, but then came the moment when we had to make the difficult choices all anthologists face. We wanted to give a meaningful sample of the writers we chose and this could only be done by narrowing the number of poets.

We avoided the temptation to use criteria such as gender, race or location, which might have helped us with our choices at the expense of merit. Instead we approached each submission with the sensibilities of ardent and open-minded poetry readers. We were looking for poems that delighted, startled and engaged us, poems that revealed joy in language and touched us with the wonder of what poetry can be. We set aside issues of subject and form, in favour of a more general belief poetry is an intimacy that connects. It should move us to a heightened state of awareness and at the same time remind us of our shared humanity. It should reveal the power of common words to become numinous. The poems that follow achieve that, and some do more.

These new poets are skilful, energetic and precocious. Nadine Shelly, for instance, published a book of poetry with Exile Editions when she was only sixteen. Karen Connelly is the youngest writer to have received a Governor General's Award, in her case for nonfiction, and she also won the Pat Lowther Award for her first book of poetry. Evelyn Lau won the Milton Acorn Memorial Award for her first poetry collection and was shortlisted for a Governor General's for her second. Others in the anthology have been acknowledged by a profusion of honours including the Gerald Lampert Award, the Bronwen Wallace Award, the BC Book Award for Poetry and The League of Canadian Poets' national prize. They are as eclectic as they are talented. Their subjects range from the impossibility of finding the perfect man, to the infanticide of a pet rabbit, to the luscious lexicon of a blackberry bush; from one of King Solomon's wives, to Alice out of Wonderland, to a baby in a jar. Most of the poets, however, come back to family in one way or another, offering the reader an intimate portrait of mothers and fathers as seen through the eyes of children who grew into poets and chose to tell the tales. But then, how could you not tell the story of a mother whose horse lifts her by the hair or a father who dances his daughter into the fire?

The free-verse lyric poem with an underlying narrative continues to be the most popular form with this generation as with the last. Once again we were reminded what a wide and complex range lyric poetry can embrace. Though most of the poems come closer to ordinary speech than song, we favoured those which also resonated with music, the cadences and repetition of sounds adding a sumptuous richness to the colloquial voices. We saw few prose poems in the submissions, although some are included here, and almost nothing of the new formalism beyond a single sestina and ghazal, and a few sonnet variations.

Although we didn't consciously arrange it, we were pleased with the multicultural and regional mix we ended up with. The anthology is truly a Canadian one, spanning the country from sea to sea; balancing what lies between are poems about a salmon fisherman on the West Coast and a cod fisherman on the East. For some reason, more poets from British Columbia submitted to the anthology than those from other provinces, and both before and after our selection the women outnumbered the men. Several of the poets, including Sally Ito, Greg Scofield and Marisa Alps, bring their racial heritage to the forefront.

This is a pragmatic group of tree planters, journalists, college teachers, fishermen, publishers' assistants and secretaries who keep their day jobs yet continue to make poetry a central concern of their lives. Their voices are often daring, revealing and sometimes refreshingly outrageous. There's anger in some of these poems, but there's never cynicism or cold objectivity. Rather, these poets are unapologetically engaged with words and the world. There seems to be a new romanticism, a faith in the power of poetry to rekindle, redeem and renew. Without a doubt, these are writers "breathing fire and poetry" into the future.

— LORNA CROZIER AND PATRICK LANE

Marisa Alps

Marisa Alps grew up on Quadra Island, BC. She has a BA from Simon Fraser University, and has been broadcast on CBC radio reading her poetry and talking about her Eurasian heritage. Her work also appears in *Swallowing Clouds*, an anthology of Chinese-Canadian poetry (Arsenal Pulp Press). Currently, she lives on BC's Sunshine Coast and is working on a manuscript of poems.

Lionel Trudel

Calligraphy Lessons

"Hold the brush like you have an egg in your palm," Mr. Pang said to me
and I tried, cross-eyed with concentration. Once a week after my dance
class my mother and I would squeeze into this small room off Little
Panda and with a half-dozen others try to please Mr. Pang: ink on our
fingers, paper like dry leaves, the colour of sticky rice. The stiff
hairs of bamboo brushes turned soft from resting in our
shallow water dish (my characters were always stunted and unsure
not what he wanted, long fluid brushstrokes), he taught me how to
write my Chinese name   one - two - three   no!   don't
stop mid-stroke! 安 林 trees and peace.

I never did learn calligraphy, never discovered anything but my name
and later I would mourn this loss, would want to own this skill
hang it on my wall, framed in silk and weighted. I don't think
my mother learned either, and my father and brother stayed home.

1

In Chinatown the waiters talked to her in Cantonese, and although my
mother understood as little as I did, she always knew what to order
what was inside the rice flour dumplings, the sweet red surprises,
brushstrokes tilting and scenting the air, hundred-year-old eggs staining
her hands.

Dancing I

One night I caught my mother dancing
she sings and cries (so long)
while winter begins to frost and snow

light on the water, her paddle cuts cleanly
she glides. All has been leading up to this
quiet in surprise
she takes it

dancing
her arms like waves
on the shore, arch and bend
but strong
as she heads into the wind
with movements like music,
this body graceful and undulating,
dancing

   (I remember coming suddenly
   into a room and catching
   my father mid-jig,
   his nervous giggle,
   his turning away)

Where did you hide the dancing before?

You brought it out once a year to be admired,
stroked it, brushed it

till your dancing glinted smooth in the sun
fine and sultry
pressing in the room's heat and soft shadows
then you put it away again
shut the drawer
until you needed it

Dancing II

You woke up from your dreams
smelled onions frying in your kitchen
and you knew
without a doubt that he was there.
seconds later
you were dancing
half-hidden by the forest that
sprouted up around you, leaves
curling from the wooden boards
moss spreading under the sink
where it was moist
and the rug in the living room
grew grass that shifted in the wind and sun
light, turned to oriental jewels

in movements soft and gentle, you
stiffened at noise
your shape transforming
into animal, one
paw lifted

and then you were bear, and swallow, and deer
no one else saw your self-shifting—
for one moment
caged but free you were scared to stop
because if you lost your

new forms
you lost
their magic, their life.

Dreams

She is beautiful, isn't she
the way she moves
toward you in the night
makes you gasp
for breath
moves past the sweat
that gathers along your hairline
into a larger space
the deeper place
of dreams

And when you turn
into her
sheets rolling back
revealing the white underside
of vulnerability
her bright pictures explode become
interruptions of time and people
hitch-hiking into darkness

this is fear
this is beauty
and she will not stop
for anything.

Spring Falls

To Meiling

I cried when
you said how waiting for death
was like waiting for birth—
the tension, the pain, the knowledge
that you are present for a
momentous occasion
something that will change
your life forever

while we walk in the garden
you show me
the narcissus,
the unfurling buds of the cherry tree still
sleeping
the crocus that has already lived
its short life
purple and orange petals
crushed to the ground

I am amazed to see how things
have and have not changed
inside, we drink tea and laugh
walk around the space
where my father lived
pour a cup for him too, his
rings still on the table
interlocking circles darkening
the wood

outside, spring falls
like rain
the flowers push up

demanding their space
their beauty in this fragile world—
faces
open to the sky

Stephanie Bolster

Stephanie Bolster's poetry has appeared in many journals, including *The Malahat Review*, *Prairie Schooner*, *Grain*, *The Fiddlehead* and *Poetry Canada*. She has an MFA in Creative Writing from UBC and participated in the Banff Centre's 1994 Writing Studios. Born and raised in Vancouver, she currently lives and writes in Quebec City.

Come to the edge of the barn

Come to the edge of the barn the property really begins there,
you see things defining themselves, the hoofprints left by sheep,
the slope of the roof, each feather against each feather on each goose.
You see the stake with the flap of orange plastic that marks

the beginning of real. I'm showing you this because
I'm sick of the way you clutch the darkness with your hands,
seek invisible fenceposts for guidance, accost spectres.
I'm coming with you because I fear you'll trip

over the string that marks the beginning, you'll lie
across the border and with that view—fields of intricately
seeded grain & chiselled mountains, the cold winds
already lifting the hairs of your arm—you'll forget your feet, numb
in straw & indefinite cow dung, & be unable to rise, to walk farther.

My fingers weave so close between yours because I've been there
before, I know the relief of everything, how it eases the mind to learn
shapes it has not made, how it eases the feet to know the ground
will persist. See those two bowls of milk, just there,

on the other side of the property line, they're for the cats
that sometimes cross over & are seized by sudden thirst, they're
to wash your hands in. Lick each finger afterwards. That will be
your first taste, & my finger tracing your lips will be the second.

(*The first line is one of John Ashbery's "37 Haiku."*)

Many Have Written Poems about Blackberries

but few have gotten at the multiplicity of them, how each berry
composes itself of many dark notes, spherical,
swollen, fragile as a world. A blackberry is the colour of a painful
bruise on the upper arm, some internal organ
as yet unnamed. It is shaped to fit
the tip of the tongue, to be a thimble, or a dunce cap
for a small mouse. Sometimes it is home to a secret green worm
seeking safety & the power of surprise. Sometimes it plunks
into a river and takes on water.
Fishes nibble it.

The bushes themselves ramble like a grandmother's sentences,
giving birth to their own sharpness.

Picking blackberries must be a tactful conversation
of gloved hands. Otherwise your fingers will bleed
the berries' purple tongue; otherwise the thorns
will pierce your own blank skin. Best to be on the safe side,
the outside of the bush. Inside might lurk

nests of yellowjackets; rabid bats; other,
larger hands on the same search.

The flavour is its own reward, like kissing the whole world
at once, rivers, willows, bugs and all, until your swollen
lips tingle. It's like waking up
to discover the language you used to speak
is gibberish, and you have never really
loved. But this does not matter because you have
married this fruit, mellifluous, brutal, & ripe.

Whose Eyes

The expression in the eyes of Dodgson's photographs
of the real Alice is nothing but
seduction. He would not have
used the word; he might have said: *Pretend*
you want something very badly, but someone
will not give it to you, though there is a small
chance they might. He might have called it
hinting, might have tilted
the head down so the eyes gazed from beneath
shadowed lids while he murmured:
There, you are beautiful.

For this Oxford don with that huge contraption of a camera
& a large nose, this shy man
with the waves in his hair, she may have endured
a long monotony of posing, given
these looks to enter stories.
Pretend you are the Queen of Hearts, in a huff—
and through these new eyes she saw her servants
busily painting white roses red, hedgehogs & flamingoes
at her service.

Nestled close against the lens,
he would have stammered: Yes,
yes, as he draped the dark
cloth over his head. Yearned to crawl into the tunnel
of the aperture, find the place where her
image waited with its long-lashed eyes,
all in black & white, able
to be touched, while the little girl had already
giggled and flounced outside to play hide & seek
in the red garden.

Alice's Dreamed Garden Contained in a Vase

When you realize the blooms of iris are no longer
blooms but shrivelled bits of fading purple, not *something*
but what's left after something's gone, you think about your hands.
How much more can they curl into themselves and still be
themselves, how much more can the veins swell
before they become dark stems?

Something will end all this—
an explosion inwards of the blood, stoppage of the heart.
Then you will be planted, the bones that were your hands
caught in their own clasp, wedding band
a loop of metal falling.

But if *Reginald goes first*, if his dear hands are locked away,
then yours will hold the smallness of themselves
long before that last clutch. Those hands that cupped butter
to your mother's chin, held Dodgson's hand on garden walks,
your sister's while her young body withered from within.

If *Reginald goes first*, then your hands will be
touched with no imagination. They will be only flesh
on bone the way iris is only
a cluster of purple petals on a stem prone
to leaning, garden rakes abandoned in
some place long past tending.

Transformations

Tell the story from the caterpillar's point of view
and the movement would be slower, measured
in inches, the length of the tea table lasting for days.
In the pool of tears the caterpillar would likely have drowned.
And when the Queen of Hearts screamed
he would have curled into himself,
inert on the grass, nosed by hedgehogs.

We would see Alice, her stubby, shrunken arrival
at the mushroom site, buckles & patent shoes creased
as she peered up to meet
the caterpillar's gaze, light glinting
off the top of her head, her eyes
guarded against too much curiosity.
She would never devour, only
sip, nibble.

But Alice's "tomorrow"
& the caterpillar's would each be portrayed
as a Turner painting, vague & stormy,
with a light in the distance. It could be
an oncoming train, or a newly emerged butterfly
sucking a *hookah*, or the end
of the tunnel. It could be a girl's teeth
smiling when she'd really rather not.

11

Lesley-Anne Bourne

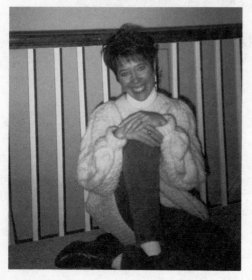

Lesley-Anne Bourne has published two books of poetry, *The Story of Pears* and *Skinny Girls*, both with Penumbra Press. She received the 1994 Air Canada Award, administered by the Canadian Authors Association, for a promising writer under thirty. She lives in Charlottetown.

Think of Him

on a raft. Blue July
above as he stretched
a muscled arm over
her back.
Waves the boat tossed

loosened his grip and
the hand drifted down
where her bathing suit
stopped. The Mullens
inside making lunch.

He swam the cold lake
a lot the summer
they were sixteen. At night

the mosquitoes sung
when he snuck into

the guest cottage.
The dark smell of moth balls
and oiled skin.
He said he loved her
if he could

pull the sheet back.
A trout on the wall above.
Yard lights shined
the glass eyes. They were
still on the raft,

the small bed rolling
under his weight. She believed
water would wash over
everything or she could always
come up for air.

Cars and Fast-Food

He was too fast Friday nights
after twelve cans
when he drove her home.
His construction hands. She
loathed the green vinyl
inside, the windows that wouldn't
roll down. The ice-packed streets of
her neighbourhood became his
after 3 a.m. —he'd set slalom
courses through trees,
over well-cared-for lawns,
barely missing a porch.

He wanted her
to relax, let go he said
of the door, move over
so he could steer. She'd light
his cigarette and hope
her house was on the other side.
A ton of metal
she couldn't get past.
His football shoulders
played to win,
he drove her.
No cops ever caught
the red lights, the railway tracks
he risked. And after,
he'd say, 'Let's go eat
at the Blue Haven,' as if
everything was still open.

Risks

She meets a boy
she skiied with
long ago. He is
a big city lawyer now,
an expensive briefcase.
In the Renaissance cafe they are

tables side by side.
He hears her
tell the waiter
their hometown and smiles
the perfect opening.
She remembers

his hair lighter and how
he was fat. Still
she wanted to kiss him
on the trail off
the main hill. She held
his hand going up

the T-bar. No one else
liked him, he acted
smart and so
she got laughed at too.
And now he's indifferent
to risks she took

back then, the howls
of her girlfriends
in the washroom
or the school dance when
he put his hand down
her jeans' back pocket

slow dancing. She knows
she even closed her eyes
once or twice
as the song went on
and when she opened
them their classmates stared

shocked. Tonight he is
asking in cavalier tones
is she divorced too
and though he is thinner and
handsome some ways,
she realizes, that night

in the middle of a winter
street where he

bruised her mouth
with his chin toward
a kiss, was as good
as it's going to get.

Night Before

The night before the worst
possibility, he goes out
while she watches
the game on TV.

A relief pitcher
jogs from the pen
just as she's afraid
the doctor tomorrow

will say something
bad. How her husband feels
is a mystery in a jazz club
downtown. She bets

he's scared—it's his
body, the lump inside
him. For once she doesn't know
the right thing, good

news not hers to say.
She'd give anything
—top of the eleventh
all tied, two on

and two out—if
the game would wind up
the way they hope.

My Mother Turns Fifty

Today. As I'm dialing
I think about death
the way she won't
let her telephone voice
tell all. We try to talk
weather there, how awful
it is sleeting like it has
today of all days. I wish
I were with you, I say
glad I'm not. My sister
gave an expensive sweater.
I mailed a poetry book
signed by a friend who writes
things about her mother
mine won't want. I
sent a photo as well—
me at twenty-five,
half of what she is, oh, to be
her the days she swam
in Muskoka to the raft
with us. She wore
a bikini back then, the lake
puddled warm on the wooden boards.
I wanted to be her
mermaid, the one who gave life
when kissed.
Under the four o'clock sun I
put my hand on her
thigh, little older than mine
now, the hot brown skin, her
suntan oil smell, the
long wet hair. Miles away today

I'm dreaming she's lying
on the bottom, half-buried
in sand and shells and weed—
this voice diving in
to salvage her.

In the Past

ten years her father's seen her die
almost. He still asks why
did she starve so long?
How? Under the hospital window
he thought she couldn't hear

When can I *trust*
her again? The nights
he'd sign her out for baseball
games in Lee Park, returning
at ten to the fourth floor

as if normal. His heart
breaking each time they passed
icecream stands. Or lunch hours
he walked from the office
to watch her not eat. In the past

ten years she's come back
a pound at a time.
He pretends not to count.
Playing catch in the yard
when she visits, they throw

fast balls and curves
without effort or hurting
each other that bad.

Thea Bowering

Thea Bowering is a student and writer from Vancouver. She was an exchange student for one year at Aarhus University in Denmark, and is completing her studies at Simon Fraser University. Her previous poetry and prose have been published in *The Lyre*, Capilano College's student literary magazine, and in the Ottawa magazine, *Free Verse*.

Conjuration.

Shane flew thru open doors like the rites of spring
I saw cherry blossoms ascend from his fingertips!
magician gestures twist
mere balloons into wonderful doggy shapes,

the fabulated wrist
signaling a second of disbelief
in the eyes of the birthday kid
waiting in suspense for the promised.

And the magic was still there
in the candy aisles of the liquor store
lemon gin to a dancing ear
pearls found glowing in the guttered
cement curbs of a wet night fall.

There is no special reserve for invention.
It is right in the yellow heart of the lemon gin gold
or pulled from your breast pocket
a stream of giant hankies
in knotted gasps of colour.

Women in the duty free.

Women in the duty free
their noses tentatively snoofing
for essences in *Obsession*, *Eternity*, *Escape*
wishing for a captive word.
Think of me this way it says
passing glittering cashiers.

Femininity mingles in air, a kind of chaos
shooting each other on wrists.
The end inevitably
a disappointing trace of alcohol
while feet spread wide by the sample testers,
knees like a goal tender's bent
to balance on the rocking ferry floor.

No Ophelia on the river surrounded in blossoms nope.
The stink of rotting petals in water is not sweet.
But isn't this how they'd have you imagine
perfume is made?
Squeezed from white linen and opium,
petals on water,
a sinking maiden.

kitchen familiarities:

Sitting in someone else's kitchen
enjoying hard wood floor
on the balls of my feet
glancing
at dishes I won't have to wash,
I listen to someone else's quietness.

Things have been dropped carelessly during moments
I don't know of
      dishtowel,
                    spoon,
small
black
book.

The dishes had their place on the shelves
long before I came to this kitchen.
They will be put away, in ritual pattern,
long after I stop coming here.

The pattern is unimportant to the owners of the dishes.
They are hardly aware of it.
They rub a steel pot,
dry it,
place it in its spot
while they talk; lilting laughter of
which they are unaware is also
a pattern someone may notice,
and think delightful.

They do not have to ask
"where does this go?"
and they will take everything when they go,
and not look back at yellow rings left on shelves.

21

They will find new spaces to put things,
spaces that seem obvious.

———————————————

Men arrange kitchens beautifully.
The corkscrew where you expect it to be
There is always Earl Grey tea around somewhere
honey and milk.
Unexplainable, sexy tenderness in
knives, forks, pottery plates, the
kettles, large coffee mugs of men.

We watch you intently.
You move gracefully around your kitchens.
To a drawer for spoon,
up for sugar,
to stove for boiling water.
A hand unfolds here, feet shift weight, hips move
from one counter to the next.
We hold our breaths—
you don't think of your kitchen
you are just in it.
You just need a cup of coffee in the morning;
it is not ballet.

You would be embarrassed if you knew how we saw you.
Wonder
of movements in the kitchen space
which separates us.
We will learn where the sugar is kept.
We might eventually reach for it with ease
But we know it will be there long after
we have stopped reaching for it.

We will love your kitchen,
think of it at nights

spoon, sugar, cup, kettle
shiny off-white wood.
You will think of it seldom,
form new patterns:
cup, spoon,
kettle, sugar;
these are your tools.

lost in the transaction:

Rape doesn't happen in Denmark smiley boy on his bicycle tells
you while he holds out his hand, and touches your shoulder, with the
tips of his fingers as you ride your bikes parallel on the way there.
In the university pretty potted plants keep sitting on the window
ledges and for some reason no one steals them. You pass where
people have left their scarves and mittens all over public places and
other people have hung them up cheerfully on staircase banisters
and bushes, even the ones that aren't disgusting colour combinations,
to be reclaimed and rejoiced over.

But when you buy the bread and beer on the way there, the
price ends up being 85 kroner and 95 ore, well there is no ore coin
under 25 so you ultimately lose that 5 and it's just another time this
happens and you don't think about it. So why exactly have you
ridden to his kitchen with the advertisement section of the
newspaper in the corner to drink this enormous can of beer just
because earlier you enjoyed turning stingy hallway furniture upside
down in the psychology institute calling it art, standing back rubbing
the old chin and critiquing its worth like the pros. Trusting your
laughter was something in common.

Well that doesn't seem to make much difference now that you're
holding onto his bookshelves with your toes because this hurts and
when will it end and what a strange time to think about being eight
or so, naively soaking rose petals in water and trying to bottle the

rotten stuff, cause you were sure that's how it's made, in your mom's old empty perfume bottles she kept wistfully in her underwear drawer, and when those ran out you went on to old jam jars and thought you could sell the stuff on the street like Lucy Van Pelt sells psychiatric advice.

It never crossed your mind he might have an ac/dc t-shirt nursed from teenagehood, unknown to you, unmothered with wrinkles and faded gray and blue cracking iron-on under that black sweater which, now that you come to think of it, a lot of types could wear not just the interesting ones. Who knew? puffs of animal hair on his shoulders, or a thrust could stop your heart—suddenly feeling the order of things. And you remember once as a kid, when seeing a furniture ad claiming slashed prices, deciding that you would one day sell large sofas for a penny each. And what are you doing here? on your back, condoms breaking, when just last week you felt like such a gentleman, the back of your coat flapping in triangles about your knees in the wind.

Tim Bowling

Tim Bowling was born, raised, and lives in Ladner, BC, where he works as a deckhand on a Fraser River gillnetter. The winner of the 1994 National Poetry Contest, he has had his poems published in many journals and magazines, including *Canadian Forum*, *The Fiddlehead*, *Grain*, *Poetry Canada* and *Queen's Quarterly*. His first collection, *Low Water Slack*, was published by Nightwood Editions.

The Last Sockeye

for my brother

Always I think of the last sockeye,
the one in late October; blind,
blood-red, half-rotted, so far
from the creeks of spawning,
it just lay beside our net
in the silt-grey water—confused
or resting, we couldn't say—
then with one weak push
gilled itself
so we had to roll it in.

The last of its kind for the season;
most had died, or spawned and died,

at least a month before:
I could not gaff it.
We stood in the chill north wind, bemused,
as though we'd been given an early Christmas gift,
red-wrapped and taken
from below the mountains' undecorated evergreens;
we stared at the rotted eyes
and scales like bloodied coin,
a glove of chain-mail
after a Crusades slaughter
the living hand still inside.

Three separate instincts
and a whole long winter to forget
your drinking and failed marriage
my loneliness and too often
days of great despair
over things I cannot change

and always the gap between us
as wide as the gap
between the sockeye and its goal;
three separate instincts
with nothing to win
three separate species:
I don't remember what we said
or even if we spoke at all
but the salmon, at least,
knew what it wanted,
so I gave it back to the river,
blind, rotted, and doomed,
I gave it back

while we stood in the stern like the last men
and watched the bloody hand of the year wave goodbye

Young Eagle on a Piling

We had thought to drift so far
meant no witness but the wild sea
and the last glazed gape
of dying salmon slicked
in their own blood at our feet;
we had thought to feel our bones
pull anchor from our flesh
as shore and safety fell away
meant an isolation known
perhaps to saint and sacrifice
but not to common men:
black clouds scraped across the sky
behind which a few stars in
their pale youth stared down
pitiless. Yet we could not accept
the casual coming of the night,
how it deepened so slowly
like the blush on a grape,
how it swept over the waters
in a silent tide, dragging
its corkline of distant worlds,
its giant ghostly buoy;
we could not believe in death
of such a soft arrival

Until at the river's final marker,
a decayed piling looming just beyond
our bow, like a scorched stake
kindled by the flesh of suns,
we felt the hour's essential hunger
pierce our skin, we felt
for the first time
our slicked hearts thrashing

in our hands: there,
calmly perched against the wind,
his feathers ruffled like the water's surface,
a young eagle looked beyond our selves
to the darker simpler facts
of fear, and what they meant
to his survival. For only a second
out of the gloom, we met
his steady yellow gaze, beacon
to a shore we had no wish
to touch, and then, as quick,
the night consumed the piling
and its patient guest

Later, the net picked up at last,
the still catch gasping in the stern,
we trained a spotlight on his perch
but he had gone,
dark ash of the day's staked sun
scattered in the storm,
raised anchor of the seeking blood
dragged across the stars,
black soul, pure need,
the truth our pretty lives
had drifted from

Tides (A Poem to Myself)

Steal a rowboat tonight. Unlasso the mooring
that holds you to the shore. It's spring and
twilight and all the flowering cherries of
the earth have come on like pink streetlamps
to shed softness on your rainsweet ways
to the riverbank,

but do not linger as you might have
once, dreaming of French girls in their boudoirs
powdering a desired cheek; leave that
for the hockeymad boys levelling the grass
of vacant lots with scarred Sherwoods,
let them practise the loneliness
they need to perfect;
yours is already a statue marbled
by the moon, and stands in a field
where owls drag the darkness for suicides
and where the grave of each small shadow
they leave in the night
fills slowly with bones.

Instead, take the oars gently
as you would the arms of someone you love;
they're weightless, but the journeys inside
whisper with a heft only the intimate touch
understands. Now plunge your own still map
into the drifting ashes, and row:
if the oarlocks creak, imagine doors opening;
if your rhythm is off, keep time
to the motes of dusk that tap your skin.
Soon, no doubt, a muskrat will splash
down from the marsh, one black key played
on the piano, and a heron will hang
its soft, blue linen from the first faint star:
when this happens, do not be distracted;
arrive at the place where the current
runs strongest. And rest.

Breathe deep. Let darkness sink the world.
Let the stevedoring wind
load a freight of scentless blossoms
in the stern. The tides will bear it to the sea

and, somehow, bring you back alone,
with the blood your heart has yet to make
compass and anchor
for every mortal voyage
your unheld arms have just begun to dream.

Snowy Owl After Midnight

I like to believe he waits for me
in the dark pines along the river,
eyes trained on the porchlight
of my house;
I like to believe his blood stirs
at my presence, in a way unknown
to him, but that he also understands
the heightened smell of joy and fear
my bones give off
as I shut the door behind me·
and plunge into the stars.

It is so quiet at this hour,
just the two of us awake,
each hunting in his way
the small gifts of the night,
what he seeks in the long grass
and marshes, what I seek
in the soft, unpeopled silence:
at first I thought I followed him
along the dyke and through the fields,
privy to a ritual strange and
wild in its solitude;
now I'm not so sure.

For miles
he wings above my shoulder

quick and small as those moons
we watched in childhood
from the backseats of our parents' cars,
those moons that always raced us home,
that we could never lose
and when I stop, he's there,
settling on a fence-post or piling,
diving behind a clump of trees;
never a shriek from the grass
never a word from my throat;
we have circled each other's silence
this way for months.

Again, tonight, I wonder
what he would tell me if he could;
would he say the blood that calls him
to the earth is a blood
he does not understand?
Under these drumming wings I wonder
what death does he expect
my clipped, pale hands to make?

I would say to him now,
this blank page riffling in the night,
this beating heart of a snowman
extant from some boyish dream,
brother, I have stopped my ears against
the blood that calls me to the earth
but I will move here with you
in its dark and silent flowing
as long as breath is given
and your vigil burns white fire in the trees.

Sioux Browning

Sioux Browning was born and raised in the East Kootenays of BC. She has left many times but always returns to hang out in the mountains. Browning has a BA in English from the University of Victoria.

The Perfect Ten

I want a man who will wear a baseball cap
every day of his life — long past the time
when his last strand of hair has fallen out.

I want a man for whom the four food groups
are meat and potatoes, barley and malt.

I want a man with a cherry red 4 by 4
jacked up to the point that I need a ladder to get in it,
with fuzzy seats and blue sex lights lining the dash
and a hockey stick in the gun rack.

I want a man who will take me mud-bogging,
or at the very least to the monster truck exhibition
down at the stadium.

I want a man who will call me "mother" at home and
"the little woman" around his friends;
who will pat me on the butt in public and announce
I seem to be gaining a few.

I want a man who is not afraid to let his Molson muscle
hang over the front of his speedos;
who will wander around the house in his underwear
with his hand stuck down the front, scratching absently
as he looks for the T.V. Guide.

I want a man who refers to motorcycles as crotch-rockets,
who thinks a romantic proposal is, "Hey baby, let me slip
you my hot beef injection."
who cleans his fingernails with his teeth,
and who can hit any moving dog at thirty paces by flicking
a twist-cap by his ear.

I want a man who thinks Jean-Claude Van Damme is an
acting tour de force.

I want a man who thinks tour de force is a bicycle race in Europe.

I want this man because he is so hard to find. His kind
all seem to be taken by women luckier than me.
Women who didn't waste their time looking
for someone better, first.

Dark

The moon's cool wind on my clothes
the stars—tiny pearls of milk upon a cat's tit,
the meadow, beaten down by the wings of swallows
and the weight of
summer flowers

The forest sounds
like someone approaching in the dark
touch-touch, touch-touch
Somewhere in the grasses in
the summer flowers
coyotes are singing

The night has severed us
the curve of your leg gone
from beneath my thigh

Like a bobcat
startled off her kill
we have been startled off each other
padding silently apart

Striking Camp

I gut a salmon
hang the pink flesh over embers,
wash some socks,
wring them and hang them
over branches to dry.
I eat and go to bed,
watch the condensation form
on the nylon of the tent
in the half-light.

In the morning, the socks are gone
and strips of smoked salmon hang in their place.
The mist confuses everything.
Ravens hop around the fire circle,
scratching at the dirt.

Darkness sinks into the lake,
unsounded, unreflecting

swallower of salmon, socks and ravens.
The kayak hesitates
at the water's edge.
Once on the water I am kept
company by birds.
Turning, I no longer see the shore.

Suzanne Buffam

Born in Montreal in 1972, Suzanne Buffam now lives in Vancouver with a view of the docks, the mountains and BC Place stadium. Her work has appeared in various journals, a chapbook with Panarky Press, and the anthology *Eye Wuz Here* (Douglas & McIntyre). Her future plans: to drive through Hope with the windows down, give up making excuses.

---

drive thru

at the ladysmith dairy queen i want to get out
& stretch, but my dad says we've only got time
for the drive thru today, watching the snow
pile up on the road, he says it's best to keep moving

& i can't help thinking of you

as we pass strips of motels, their parking lots empty,
plastic vacancy signs that promise a room with a view
of the highway.

he says, d'you know what you want? & i want
to tell him he won't want to know,
that i'm thinking he's right; it's best
to keep moving.

i think of weekends you've planned for us
but not carried out
& imagine frozen swimming pools fenced in around back,
adult cable tv & thick shag carpet underfoot.

but it's not you
that i want to bring to this place,
to this drive thru town on the edge
of highway one, to the seaview resort
the port, or the oceanfront. you ·
who would always rather fly, who won't let me sing
along with the radio, who turns off
the light to make love.

      as my dad shifts gears past the bar
in this town, i'm singing off-key in the shower
of a room with a view at the seaview resort
with some random lover—his hands on my back
slipping with soap. driving thru
his bones like a car thru this town, fast &
laughing with the wind in my face,
feeling the bumps on his spine like the
ridge in the road, his quick breath
on my neck coming at me like the rise & fall
of the price of gas between here & where
we are heading.

Half-light

In the green half-light of three a.m.
my brother wakes me, pulls my slumbering body
into the yard to see the rabbits being born.

They emerge all wet and pink as finger
tips nestled into sawdust beneath

their mother—one, two, then three

naked bodies in the sudden beam
of my brother's flashlight. We hold
our breath as her small eyes take us

in, red in the light, full of fire,
and there is a moment, heavy as
the moon, when we know it is too late

to retreat, unsee, resume our innocent
beds. The mother's eyes angry
as she hunches up and turns away,

leaves us watching, the wind
cold through our nightclothes, as she swallows
up her children—one, two, then three

wriggling bodies disappear into her tiny
sharp-toothed mouth, the flashlight
dropping to the grass at our feet.

Homing

these are decisions I can make;
how hot the shower, how long
the silences. I love the sound
of doors slamming, the colour
red, the crest of anger
as it swells before the calm
blind pain. I quit
the piano, horses, the ocean, gave up
arguments, the desire to dream
of becoming everything, but not
desire itself. I can get in my car
and turn the key, I can go this far.

but the night is dark and I follow
wherever the pavement suggests, my hands
steering their way towards nothing
discernible. a pair of dumb pigeons
who have lost all sense of direction.
somehow they always find their way
through the streets, deliver me
safely back to myself, still
wedged behind the wheel, watching
the rain as it mists and collects,
as it mists and collects on the windshield,
and I wait for something
inside me to move.

Astronomical Love

Look! It's the Little Dipper, you say, pointing out the cluster
of scars, moonpale and shiny as a dime, that curve up
around my ankle-bone, dip low and deep as my heel.

You like to examine me this way, chart your travels
over my body with your naked eye open.
Up by my pelvis you discover Cassiopeia, The Chained
Lady, matching up the picture in the small dark
book by your bed with the appendix scar I tried so long to hide
with high-cut panties and one-piece bathing suits.

The moons of Jupiter circle my wrist, waxing and waning
in the crescent shapes of teeth, where a plate-glass window
tried to swallow my fist.

On a good night, which is rare, you can make out Cancer
clustered on my collarbone, where I was scratched
by a pet rabbit, inches from where my heart should be.

And Betelgeuse, that one bright star in Orion's belt,
shines from my navel, the celestial equator that cuts
me in two. You spread me out before you

like a map, and telescope into my body,
hoping to reach galaxies invisible
to the naked eye of man, while what I want is to interpret
these signs, line the moons of me up with my stars
and understand where we are going, where we both are
coming from.

At Least

First the african violet, its soft
purple flower and bruised
downy leaves arching to light.
Then the fig tree's flooded
roots rotten in soggy soil, crisp
brown leaves all over the floor,
like a knocked-apart house
of cards. The nasturtiums knotted,
coiled in on themselves, took on
that universal yellow
warning—the jaundiced whites
of a dying man's eyes.

Goldfish rose one by one, their bellies
like hot air balloons, to the surface
of the small glass bowl, unnaming
themselves as they came;
the rabbit froze stiff in his cage
overnight, dish full of food
at his nose; a hamster named after the French
jazz singer who killed herself with too much
fast living; frogs, crabs, the snake

that kept trying to escape—
all left the house in little cardboard
coffins, just the size
for a pair of shoes.

And of course the bigger inexplicable
ones: golden retriever, siamese cat,
horse that died with its head in my lap.

                    Now I want to perform
an autopsy on every living thing as it enters
the rooms of my life, isolate the cause
before it dies, at least
be able to name it: how the frog that sings
and sings through the night
becomes a waxy stone, my love,
a cage of danger.

anticipating rain

do you know the sound of my footsteps in the hallways
of your bones? yours echo in mine like a small

departure, a slowly concluding paragraph.
how the little frog sings in his jar on the mantle,

longing for trees, the excruciating splendor of
leaves. my flesh, wanting to close around your

name like the gently folding earth. my heart.
a smooth little stone. a window pane. a jar.

i will leave the light turned on for you,
above the sleeping butterfly faces of our children

how they flutter & fold, their tiny wings
unable to ride the long night into your vanishing

sunrise. o the enduring unendurable rain. how softly
a finger traces my palm, like a river, flooding.

how trapped the little frog; how alone in this
dark, pressing down on me like the palm of a hand.

Alison Calder

Alison Calder grew up in Saskatoon but is currently working on a PhD in English at the University of Western Ontario. She has had both poetry and prose published in Canadian magazines such as *Grain, Dandelion* and *Books in Canada*. Current projects include completing her thesis, finishing a full-length poetry manuscript, and learning to fly-fish.

Imagine a picture

Imagine a picture of your sister or your daughter
and stretch it out. Do not stop pulling.
Stretch until the bones jut, until the body
reveals the frame. Stretch until all you see
are bones and eyes. This is a woman
who sends herself to sleep by counting ribs.
Rolls of quarters fit inside her hipbones.
Her elbows are as sharp as the corners of a mirror.
At night she dreams herself a feast.
The first dish is her thigh. The second is her belly.
All day she devours herself.

Imagine a picture of your sister or your daughter
and crumple it. Fold until she is doubled,
trebled into herself. Continue until all you see

are the folds of her clothing. This is a woman
who wears many layers. Other people's voices
fit inside her mouth. When asked her name
she says nothing. At night she dreams
a flood and a throatful of water.
At night she dreams a fire and herself
burned away. She writes

> I *am undead.*
>
> *Mirrors do not show me*
>
> *and sunlight marks my skin.*

Imagine a picture of your sister or your daughter
and tear it so many times
that some pieces become invisible.
Give them away to men you meet.
It does not matter who. This is a woman
who needs men's hands to put her together.
At night she dreams herself naked on a stage.
In the orchestra there are one thousand mirrors.
All night she tries to reassemble herself.
All day she tries to remember her reflection.

Tie me to the place

I stand with a man with whom I have been living.
He holds me back against his chest.
There is no good reason I should hate him.

We stand at the edge of a field. Below us
the river valley snakes and turns upon itself.
Far away is the reflection of the sky.

I see this like a movie. The panoramic prairie
curves like a backdrop. There is a dark patch

on the canvas but the storm may not arrive.
There is no reason to believe it will come this way.

The prairie is tricky like that. You think you see
forever but sometimes you see too far. What you think
is going to happen sometimes doesn't.
There is no accounting for the weather.

I say this is a movie but it is a still life.
I am sometimes tricky like that. The sun is out
and I am shivering. The wind pushes
and nothing is moving. Above the ground
the aspens are trembling.

Lately she can't stand

Lately she can't stand to be touched,
doesn't like the dog looking
when she gets out of the bath.
She dresses herself, layer
on layer, feels small
in her clothes and ugly without.
She looks in the mirror
sees only the cracks
and seven years bad luck.
Last year she stuffed wet towels
under the door to keep the dust out.
Last year she dyed her hair,
but nothing changed either way.

Sometimes she thinks of leaving,
tests the idea like she tests the ice
on the slough behind the house.
In town she watches men
watch young women home

for Christmas, twenty years ago
they would have been married,
would have been. She wishes
blonde hair and blue eyes
and a walk that said she knew
what she would do, forever.

Back in the bathroom
she puts her husband's razor
back on the shelf, makes sure
the childproof cap is tight
on the aspirin. The cracks
in the ice on the slough
seem wider now.
This is crazy, she says,
crazy, staring,
water dark against the ice.

Sometimes she

Though she moves alone at night
the still relief of sleep eludes her.
By day she walks across the floor as though
she has forgotten the way; as though
the kitchen is a place she had visited once
and cannot now remember.
Did she paint these walls?
Is this her handprint on the window?
There are some photos on the refrigerator
but she does not see herself in them.
Sometimes she runs outside, frightened,
turning to look at a house she doesn't know.

Something is missing or something is there.
There is no difference. When her children come

they tell her nothing has changed. She is still
the mother they came home to from school.
She says nothing but hunts for a teapot
and cups. Her children open the fridge,
complain that she has nothing to eat.
She does not ask them who they are.

She would like to take out all the furniture,
all the pictures. She would take down the curtains.
She would lock the door.
Everything would be white. Everything would be new.
There would be nothing she did not remember.

October, seeing

When you look at pictures of this time
you know when it is. People look startled,
upset in all these snaps. There are shadows
in strange places. Something is caught here.
Something besides leaves has fallen.
In the sudden cold another of your seasons
is gone. These are pictures
you might decide to keep, pull out again
and again, try to memorize what it is
you have before the next leaving.
Already you walk in snow to leave at least
footprints. Even stars are white and black now,
windows, branches, sharp frames. This is still life.
Things caught in motion, moving away.

Mark Cochrane

Mark Cochrane (b. 1965) studies gender in the English Department at UBC, and thereabouts. His poems have appeared in numerous journals across Canada, and his first collection, *Boy Am I*, was published by Wolsak and Wynn. He is a sessional instructor and former editor of *The Moosehead Anthology*. He lives in Vancouver with Barbara Parkin and their two young children.

Medea

When he kissed the other woman
under Orion's dagger on the beach
his past went nova & burst upon him.

They say it takes four years
for a marriage to expire
once you've thought its ending.

For the brilliancy of a dead star shines
on & on across the placid galaxies
with millennia-old fire, outliving

itself & watchful as a jealous
god, an eye's pinprick upon the waves.
And a posthumous love reflects itself

with an echo of that big beginning:
a false bang, fool's gold, a flying ship
& revenge with the speed of light.

Latent

Not difference between but difference within.

He is funny about locker rooms.

He cannot pretend a blind eye
to the beauty of clavicle, round pec, thick
forearm, or the gentle stretching way
a man towels his scrotum from underneath.

The heaviness of that flesh. The *gravity*.

Sometimes his envy of the other man's body
becomes erotic to him. An *aching*.

& he cannot
not tell you this now, even knowing
you may use it against him.

But this is prologue.

He has ducked into the forest
the men stalk, south of Wreck Beach
& breathless, batting at moss
has patched together
dramas, hard liaisons, a community
from the details
of their condom wrappers.

He has nodded to men on the path
but not stopped, not turned his head.

He has conversed with red naked men on driftlogs
long uncircumcised
& exposed nothing,
peeled back nothing.

He has panted up the overgrown cliff
in his pants
wanting & wanting.

He has blushed & wilted in the proud
challenge to truth of their eyes.

Once he turned his head & cruised
by accident (this is what he has said).
He turned his head, twice, & led
a boomerang-jawed Francophone
in a green windbreaker
through the streets of Montréal

only to shake him on the escalators
of an underground mall.

Later he purchased magazines of the sort
he condemns when they depict women
in their parts.

The penis is different.

When he talks with women it is ridiculous.
When he talks with women it is dangerous.
When he talks with women he agrees.

But he is a worshipper. After the mall
he zipped safe into the Métro, tunneling its head,

its lambent slit bulb, forever into.

Now the man in the windbreaker
inhabits his sleep. He takes the man
into his mouth
beside his wife.

Even in dreams
he is tight inside his clothes, tight to bursting
from this life.

Reunion

Bands of muscle   long & flanking
converge in the one well
of our hips   arched & swiveling
jointly. Even now   after the baby
politics of everyday
spit-up & curdled
sleep   there are your eyes
as you flex   eyes
sharp above me & charged
with a power that does not threaten
& we are back in the woods
where we first made love
behind the Museum of Anthropology
to re-conceive the chances of women & men
together.   Touching my teeth
is the tongue   bittersweet with smoke
that never cursed me
in the birthing room.   Thank you
for that sharing
vice-clutch of pain
your whole body squeezed me through
counting down   nails

in my back   the tearful
release of our slippery child
between us.   Thank you for showing me
your giving forth.   With the tastes
of our bodies   now   mingle
scents of our baby   milk
& maple cookie   his essence
in our hair.   You see.   After all
this nucleus remains.   At the rise
of the pubis where we meet
this perfect pivot we make
we are identical.   Admit this
as a beginning.   We roll   exchange faces
& never uncouple.   Admit this
as a possibility.   Beneath us
sandstone falls away   runnelled
into gullies by rain
that finds the sea   its wet
fingers everywhere.   We clench
& unclench like hands
like jaws.   I exhale my entire life
into your ear.   You talk
back.   We are whispering
about our son   how he sleeps
elbows akimbo
the laconic teller
in an Old West stick-up.   We miss him
already   button in a hurry
to relieve the sitter who rented
High Noon.

                We must feel our way
down a forested trail.   On the nude
beach   where women in daylight
still fear to sunbathe

alone   a constellation of bonfires
guides us from the darkness
we are guided from the darkness
by network & semaphore   the crackle
& heat of other
lovers   co-parents   women
with women & men
with men in a jubilant
matrix of difference   the shadow
& flicker of flame that kisses
each angle of our various face.

Mapplethorpe

Paint my lips. Airbrush my jawbone with talcum; my
jawbone is shaven raw-blue. Blush me, rouge me,
feather my scrolled wings of hair. I say to my wife.
I say, make me over like Mapplethorpe, lips open &
vulnerable. I say, a man like one idea of a woman.
Make me that. Later let me preen in leather, tough,
the same angle, but for now I pout into your f-stop.
Don't stop. Do me like that, yeah, like Mapplethorpe.
Closer now, cheeks lavender & brows blue, garish as
our ancestors, faces of baboons. Come to me with eyes
lined, lashes black, your broad gorgeous shoulders,
your freckled muscular neck. Let a man & a woman kiss
a woman & a man. Two palettes, & smudge, pigments
& oils: a diptych. There is gender all over our faces,
mixed up & blended over all of our faces & boy, boy am
I, am I ever, boy am I ever in love.

Karen Connelly

Kevin Porter

Karen Connelly is a Canadian writer whose first book of poetry, *The Small Words in My Body*, won the Pat Lowther award. She has also written *This Brighter Prison* and *Touch the Dragon*, a book about Thailand which won the Governor General's Award for nonfiction. She continues to write poetry and travel literature, her most recent book being *One Room in a Castle: Letters from Spain, France and Greece* (Turnstone Press). She lives in Greece.

The Word Is Absurd

Turning away is easy
after a certain arbitrary number
twelve nineteen twenty-seven.
Your lids meet each other, ravaged
flaps of black-stitched skin.
You sleep in a dry well.
You do not wonder about love,
the word is absurd,
no longer taken seriously
by yourself or by any of your friends.
It is archaic, was used by princes
and princesses in stories whose evil witch
always died.

In your stories, the evil witch
gets married.

It's easy, it gets easier.
The darkness in the room
is a weasel curled in your hands,
all muscle, fur, fang.
Through the window, the city spreads out
like a dangerous electric blanket.
Your life hangs black as a bat in the curtains,
drips into the yellow bathtub,
slithers through the intestines of the radiator.

It's not difficult, be practical.
At dawn the sun comes up, the trick works again.

You wake, your face still pressed
to the paunch of sleep.
Outside the ice melts and melts.
The sky is a ripped red sheet.

There is so much to do.
See how far the world stretches back?
It reaches deep into the sky's smooth throat.
No one chokes.
All you do is cough a little.
There are no words to justify lying there,
pretending you are dreamy-eyed.
You get up to clean the sour reek
of sex from your body.

The Ugly Mermaid

Late nights alone by water,
salted wind tears my face
like a rough-tongued cat.

The air is a black bruise,
the old lighthouse a hard lover.
Light pours from his mouth but never touches mine.
The glowing warm tongue is swallowed.

I walk away, I run, knead my feet in the dirty sand.
There are smooth chiselled bones here, bleak amethysts
of glass, fish shredded to satin tassels.
I dance over the bloated belly of a cat from the wharf.

I dream of dear Jonah and whales, but tragic miracles are rare.
I come away with kelp and jellied ghosts embroiled in my hair.
I cleave my knees on grinning rocks, rip bits of shirt and chest.
But my deepest wounds are salt stains on new leather shoes.
Later, a mad fish, I quit the sea.

My eyes are silver disks.
My fingers are stiff webs, but the water doesn't want me.
At home, I dance in my own blue arms.
I hum in a red net of hair.

My mirror sings a song:

> sea-witch, ugliest mermaid,
> a siren who seduces only herself,
> you are cast out, clenched of heart,
> you make a ragged voyage in the dark
>
> and even the sea spits you out
> like a rotten tooth.

She Returns To The Farm

Irse es morir un poco. —Aita
To leave is to die a little.

Volver es una pesadilla. Odio volver. —Noemi
To return is a nightmare. I hate returning.

I come back to an empty field,
  gray stones, warm blood beating
   through animals that no longer remember
    the smell of my skin.
And white, scapes of snow so white that my face
  is alone with them, my eyes turn to frost,
  my jaws stiffen from wind and weeping.

I have forgotten how to speak.
I cannot explain the hands that do not reach,
  the feet that walk wordless into the woods.
There is nothing here but fields and freezing steers
  and the sharp new teeth of stars.
I find the frost-plumed ribs of an old horse.
The coyotes cackle in the valley.
Even the trees, so keen and naked, are cruel.

Only the snow is not dangerous.
I touch it with my bare hands.
It is violet-skinned and cold.
I want the numbness gnawing my fingers
  to mean forgiveness

  but like the skin of a dead lover,
   the snow feels nothing,
    offers no signs.

Family Reunions

The other people quit their stone fields to come here.
They slip in from nights that even the snow abandons.
They leave ashes in their glasses
    and stains on the table.
The house is littered with bits of their hair and skin.
Bones clatter through the holes in their pockets.

All night long their hands scythe the air.
They dance their words to bloody stumps.
They bite the world and spit it out on the table,
    bitter, determined only to dirty
    every glass in these cupboards
    and break at least three.

Rage keeps them awake until night opens to dawn
                gently, like a woman's hands.
Then they unfold the worn quilts of their lives.
But their skeletons do not soften in sleep.

On waking, they are sad and broken.
They drink coffee with tongues swollen by talk and grief.
During breakfast, they seed the floor with sugar
    and spill the cream, complain that the toast
        is never warm enough.
When they leave, they walk like shadows
    who have lost their bodies to wolves.

They are the people from a history I've forgotten.
I ignore mirrors and cut my hair.
I bleach my eyes white
    to blind the other inside of me.
I wash every glass carefully,
    with a soft cloth,
    breaking nothing.

From My Father's Hand

In the pockets
I find horses' hair,
the sleek fur of a pussy willow,
old keys.

I reach into that house
        and pull out the painful creak
        of the stairs.
I find a ruined painting on a water-stained wall,
        a photograph too old to be real.
In the bottom of a drawer
there is a poem by Alexander
        —All *creatures great and small*—
                and finally I have to laugh at that.

All of these things
lie about you.
They mutter dreams to me,
words I never heard you say.
You shot the gray-hooved pony,
        axed away marsh willows.
Your keys always shone like polished copper,
                cold in my hands,
                bright as blood.

Can it be you spent
        your whole life
        killing what you didn't mean to?
The romantic wind does not
        blow any truths into my hair.
        Nothing is that easy.

But if you did live
        by drawing death,

who and what am I?
Only splinters of spruce and bone
          are left in my skin,
          slivers of the questions
     I carved in this house
          where you lived.
And here is one more, with my apologies
          tacked on like a crimson target:
               Why do I use the house, the dusty pocket,
               the past tense as if you were dead and I
               am suffering some warped sorrow?

You are there, in the field, walking home.
The red sun cuts over your head like a knife.
A clean rifle is slung over your shoulder
          and a doe rabbit hangs from your fist
                    by thin silk ears.
Her blood touches your leg like a hand.

Singing

Birds blind to glass
          are classic:
               they fly hard,
               arc wings windward, effortless—
                    then slip stunned
                         down the windows.

How many times did we do this?
They laughed at the two of us
          when we screeched and danced
          our pain on the front lawn.
Someone waved.
They thought we were singing.

But we were the ugliest crows.
We were magpies
    who lived in the alleys
    in the ravines between houses.
We were mute birds, not songbirds.
Gentle music bit our ears like ticks.

But dear sister, you are finally learning to sing.
The bones of birds are hollow.
Your ribs, played by wind, whistle high silver songs.

I live in our nest alone.
I pick through this clutch of feather and bone.
How do birds mourn?
When I cry, they think I am singing.

Love has nothing to do with closing your eyes

We begin like this:

———————————

    a needle of breath slipped into the heart
    the sheer line of air down my throat

A hundred minnows are hooked in my belly
by fingers that simply undo my coat.

Nakedness is an old blanket over solitude.
I wait for my legs to stick through the holes.
I wait for moths to land and nibble my eyes.
My hands tell the famous lies.
When I touch, I believe.

When my mind cleaves through my body
and someone hammers there,

fingers wrenching in my hair,
I dream nothing can hurt me.
I dream I am safe.

Later I remember love has nothing to do
with closing your eyes.
My body twists back into itself.
The blanket is yanked off
at the first shudder of day.
My heart is a bunch of dried berries again.
I hear the blackbirds drop down through my veins
to perch on my ribs and peck away.

How many times will this cheap miracle occur?
A shining lake of flesh rises bodily into the air
then evaporates through the door.
All the little fish slap quicksilver on the floor.

Ephemeroptera

In the beginning I was young, I whispered:

> your words echo in my body's empty well
> your voice ripens stone
> I grow cool water from rain-wet moss
> your voice runs the river emerald
> your voice sings all the flowers I cannot name

In the beginning I was very young.

We went to a lake.
The great pelicans there flew
slowly, like exhausted angels.
At night your fingers raining down my back
made me pant

Believe in this Believe in this
though it was a lie.

Yes. Our bodies lied.
Your weight crashing down
like earth from a mountainside
had nothing to do with the truth.
A natural disaster, yes, but what
was I doing in the mountains anyway?

I scraped my ankle on the rocks
watching the most brilliant rainbow
we had ever seen

but that, too, was a false sign.
I wished the cut had been deep
enough to leave a scar, I wanted
something to remember you by.
Likewise the purple palette of bruises
bitten on my shoulders, I wanted
the cries to echo in all
the hollows of our flesh.

But none of that was true enough to stay.
Now I drag a stick through the gutter
of my memory, searching for leftovers.

The mayflies.
Miniature dragons fluttered around us
those days by the lake,
clung to the cabin screens, landed in our hair.
The order *ephemeroptera*.
Born without mouths, they rise from the water
only to mate, even food unnecessary
when clean biological lust is life.
Our naked feet crushed thousands on the roads.

Cheap tar and the deaths of mayflies
designed our soles, stuck to our heels.

Now lean over, Joseph, look into the well.
Not your exquisite voice ringing there
but insects floating on the face of black water.

Michael Crummey

Michael Crummey was born and raised in Newfoundland, and now lives in Kingston, Ontario. He has published poetry and fiction in journals across the country, including *The Malahat Review*, PRISM *International*, *Quarry*, *The Fiddlehead* and *TickleAce*. He was named the winner of the inaugural Bronwen Wallace Award for poetry in 1994.

Morning   Labrador Coast

Morning   Labrador coast
my father is thirteen
no, younger still
eleven maybe twelve
shivering to warm himself in the dark

The rustle of surf behind him
the passiveness of it at this hour
the grumble of men waking early
in the shacks
the steady muffle of piss
smacking a low mound of moss at his feet

He's almost given up on childhood
works a full share on the crew

smokes dried rock-moss rolled in
brown paper out of sight of his father

Each morning he makes fists to work the stiffness
out of his hands and wrists
the skin cracked by sea salt
the joints swollen by sleep after hours of work
he soaks them in the warm salve
of his urine
shakes them dry in the cold air
and turning back to the shacks
he sees stars disappearing in the blue
first light breaking out over the water,
the dories overturned on the grey beach
waiting

Cod (I)

Some days the nets came up so full
there was enough cod to swamp the boats
and part of the catch came in with other crews
once they'd filled their own dories to the gunnels,
the silver-grey bodies of the fish rippling
like the surface of a lake
the weight of them around their legs
like stepping thigh-deep into water

Most of the work was splitting and curing
the thin gutting knife slivered up the belly
and everything pulled clear with the sound bone,
liver into the oil barrel
the thick tongue cut from the throat
and the splayed fish ready for salting then
set out on a flake to dry

This until one in the morning sometimes
a river of cod across the cutting table
in the yellow swirl of kerosene lamps
and everyone up by three or four
to get back out to the nets with the light

There was no talk of sleep when
the cod were running strong,
a few good weeks could make a season;
if they dreamt at all
in those three brief hours a night
they dreamt of the fish
the cold sweet weight of them,
fin and tail flickering in their heads
like light on the water

Cigarettes (I)

The day my grandfather died he ate
a meal of salt beef and cabbage in his
sick bed, his appetite returning for
the first time in weeks, the skin
hanging from the bones of his face
like an oversized suit.

My father had gone in to see him
earlier that morning, fifteen years old then
and thinking the old man was recovering;
they spoke for a few minutes about the cold
and about going out in the spring,
and then my grandfather asked his son for
a cigarette.

Summers, after the caplin had rolled,
the cod moved into water too deep for the traps

and the two of them would spend the days jigging,
standing at the gunnel with a line down
two fathoms, repeating the rhythmic full-arm jig
as if they were unsuccessfully trying to
start an engine;
                              mid-afternoon they'd stop to eat,
stoking the galley's firebox to stew cod's heads
and boil tea, then my grandfather would sit aft
with a pipe, pulling his yellow oilskin jacket
over his head until he was finished.
He'd known for years that my father was smoking
on the sly though he'd never acknowledged it,
hid beneath a coat to give his son
a chance to sneak a cigarette
before they got back to work.

        The air in the sick room was so cold
their breath hung in clouds between them.
My grandfather was about to die of cancer or TB
and his son sat beside the bed,
his pockets for once empty of Bugle or Target tobacco,
telling his father he had no cigarette to give him
which happened to be the truth, and felt like
a lie to them both.

Apprenticeships

How everything begins with technique
with simple repetition
the way the old masters learned
the human form by sketching it in charcoal
drawing and redrawing the hand,
the cord of muscles in the shoulder,
the thighs, the hair at the back of the neck,
until the air around the body is
luminous with the body's history,
its intent

By the age of twelve my father
could clean a fish in fifteen seconds
the gutting knife tracing the cod's spine
beneath the scaly flesh,
his blind fingers working beside the blade
pulling the back-bone clear with
the wet web of fish guts,
twelve hours a stretch he was at it some days

A hundred times now I've traced
that life and still I have not
set down what makes it important,
how little I knew of the man who
made me, who held me as a child,
the tools he started out with
his long apprenticeship

Something too obvious to be said simply
refuses to rise to the light of the words,
something as ordinary, as perfectly
proportioned as my father's hands
growing old

Rivers/Roads

*"I thought I was following a track of freedom
and for awhile it was"*
— ADRIENNE RICH

Consider the earnestness of pavement
its dark elegant sheen after rain,
its insistence on leading you somewhere

A highway wants to own the landscape,
it sections prairie into neat squares
swallows mile after mile of countryside
to connect the dots of cities and towns,
to make sense of things

A river is less opinionated
less predictable
it never argues with gravity
its history is a series of delicate negotiations with
time and geography

Wet your feet all you want
Heraclitus says,
it's never the river you remember,
a road repeats itself incessantly
obsessed with its own small truth,
it wants you to believe in something particular

The destination you have in mind when you set out
is nowhere you have ever been;
where you arrive finally depends on
how you get there,
by river or by road

The Road Home

"I think the land knows we are here,
I think the land knows we are strangers."
— AL PURDY

The highway takes you only so far,
roadsigns and pavement right to the coast of
the mainland and the island somewhere out
there beyond it, a rock cradled in fog,
a gloved fist

The ferry shoulders its way into the north Atlantic,
into rain and an easterly wind, making for
Newfoundland which is no longer my home
but the place I come from still
the place that made me
and being a stranger there now I am
more or less a stranger wherever I find myself

From the terminal in Port Aux Basques
the TransCanada works north up the coast,
picking its way through the Long Range mountains
before turning east to the interior of
spruce forests and marsh, clouds of black flies,
acres of rolling barrens
where only wind and rain and winter have
ever been completely at home;
driving through, I recognize the landscape
but not my place in it, a stiff wind
rocks the car like a small boat,
and I don't have the words to say
the countryside properly though I feel it
moving inside me, its dark strength

Coming home teaches me that I own nothing,
that there is nothing in the world
I have a claim to
though this one place has a claim to me—
turning south onto the Buchans highway
I follow the Exploits river further into bush,
through Buchans Jct. buried in waves of spruce
and past the cold length of Red Indian Lake which has
forgotten me completely since I left
here years ago . . .

Lilacs

The well is contaminated and we have to
drag a bucket of water up from the brook;
we pull handfuls of lilacs from the trees
outside the open windows and set them
in glasses through the house to mask the smell
of rooms shut up with themselves for years

There are old saucers of poison placed
on countertops and mantlepieces, spoor in the pantry
and Dad tells me how he'd chase mice through
the house with a stick when he was a boy
although it was considered bad luck for the fishing
and his father forbid killing them
during the season; in Labrador, he says
you could follow the paths they'd beaten
through the long grass in the dark
but no one raised a hand to them all summer

There are still two beds in the room
where my father was born in nineteen-thirty
and we roll out our sleeping bags there,
then walk to the corner store for food and beer;

later I watch his face in the pale light
of the coleman lantern
try to connect him to what I know of that time
dust bowl photographs, soup kitchens
stories of vagrants at back doors offering
to chop wood for a meal
but I know I have it hopelessly wrong—
he wanted nothing more for me
than that I should grow up a stranger to all this
that his be one of the lives I have not lived

　　　　　After the lights are put out
there is a silence broken only by the sounds
we make as we shift in our beds and
the occasional scuffle of mice in the hallway;
the age of the house gives a musty
undertone to the sweet smell of the lilacs
and it seems stronger in the darkness
so that I imagine I am breathing in what's left
of the world my father knew
while the part of him that has never
managed to leave here is asleep across the room

Still, I have only a vague idea of what's been lost;
my father is surrounded by more than
the simple absence I can see here
　　　　　a life he's not quite finished with going on
just beyond what he's able to touch
like the impossible ache of a phantom limb
or that craving, the automatic fumbling for
the cigarette pack he's forgotten is
no longer there

Carla Funk

Carla Funk (b. 1974) was born and raised in Vanderhoof, BC, amidst Mennonites and logging trucks. She is currently working towards a double major in English and Writing at the University of Victoria. She resides in Victoria with her husband and one-year-old daughter.

Brother and Sister

for Richard

You have his skin, sallow short-sleeved tan
melted onto the body hot Saturdays
monkey-wrenching the trucks. Your copper neck
craned over the engine,
his oil-lined palms always working to fix
what went wrong.

I have his feet, heavy toes, heels like stones,
always off-balance in the dance.
Making me his partner, he swings me
round the campfire, beer in hand, Hank Williams
blaring from the pick-up. Stumbling, he pulls me
down, my foot sliding into the hot ashes.

You have the soft spot, the bruise
on his heart, the bruise on your own.
Both of you crying that night he fell
through the bedroom window
drunk. Both of you afraid
he was going to hell.

I have the backbone, the stubborn stiff will.
After our fight, he falls asleep
outside my locked door. All night
I listen to the absence
of breath between each snore.
At the breakfast table, neither of us speaks.

We both have his hands, wide knuckles,
awkward as moths in heavy rain. His fingers
yellow and thick with arthritis, struggling
to keep his hands on the wheel
and light a cigarette at the same time.
The two of us beside him,
our hands cupped over our noses and mouths
to keep out the smell of his smoke.

The two of us, brother and sister,
carry these marks of him like wounds, burns
from a fire we were born into.

Lot's Daughter

She heard clocks deep within her belly
like night animals waiting to strike.
She was pulled in and out
of the dream where her breasts
gave milk in their sleep, and her womb
swelled tight with hunger.

In the hollow black cave
she poured the wine,
climbed across cool bedsheets,
undressed her father.

She sang softly
as she crawled up
his long hard legs, met
the grey numbness in his eyes,
her hands moving over his body,
bending and folding
his old leather skin
into newborn shapes.

Ode To Soap

The slithery lather of you, suds
blossoming on my skin, peach nectar, bluebells,
green apple, the sting of lemon. Your scent
clings behind my earlobes, melts down my neck, bubbles
over my shoulders.
                    Elusive strawberry fish, you hide
under thighs from hands that massage your sweet balm
into flesh. You who smell of satsumas unpeeling,
gardenias foaming at the petals, water lilies washing
themselves in a bath of their own perfume.
                                        Women
are drawn into rivers by your magic, their fingers
rubbing clothing against wet rock, rhythmic
as musicians welling up the sway of a waltz, the swish
and swill of you washed with the current.
I smell you everywhere.

In my grandmother's pantry, tubs of tallow and lye
pressed smooth by her hands. In bath shops

gleaming under wrap like glossed stones.
In the bedsheets my mother pins on the line,
the freshness of you filling the wind.
                              Floating moon
in a candlelit bath, you bring my husband
to bed tasting of musk and sandalwood.
You leave your scent in my baby's hair,
snowy blessings on her newborn skin.
I turn you over and over
in my palms, ritual cleansing of my body,
your slippery kisses on my skin.

Baby Stories

Beside the hanging skeleton of a horse,
there is a baby locked in the blue cupboard
at the back of my high school science room.
Stillborn at 23 weeks, he was a gift
to my teacher from his doctor-friend,
slipped into an old gallon milk jar
filled with formaldehyde.

At the beginning of every school year,
the baby is passed around the class, the students
turning and turning his cold glass womb,
white flakes shaken from the bottom,
whirling a snow scene around
his pale grey skin.

———————————

Seven months into her first pregnancy,
my grandmother's station wagon
skidded into a whiteout.
Pinned behind the steering wheel,

she hollered until a neighbour boy helped her
out of the ditch, blood dripping
down her stockings
onto the icy road.

Two days later, contractions
clamping her womb, she pushed out
her silent son, named him
Solomon, meaning peaceful
as a house of snow.

_____

My cousin Jennifer tells me about the baby left
behind the hospital where she works.
Swathed in plastic and mewing
like a kitten, still slick with birth,
breathing pale purple around the mouth.
She tells me how still the baby lay
as she carried it into the nursery,
washed its cold body, how its wrinkled hands
and feet slowly uncurled in the bathwater,
blue buds softening with the warmth.

_____

My mother's neighbour holds a funeral
for each miscarriage, marks a place in the garden
behind her house. She plants moon-daisies
for the girls, cornflowers for the boys,
presses their dried petals
into pictures for her walls.

_____

Home at Christmas, the moon unfolding
into the snowflaked dark, I lie
on my parents' lawn feeling

the movement of this baby growing
inside me. I imagine my womb a cupboard
for these frantic kicks, the turning
and turning of a body
under my hands.

He Watches my Wife Nursing;
He Avoided my Mouth

He watches my wife nursing,
her breast tucked in the baby's mouth,
top three buttons of her shirt undone.
Natural mother, he says, hungry tongue
wrapped around the words.

He avoided my mouth
in last night's dream, paralyzed tongue
when I stood tip-toe to kiss him.
Around us, a carnival of colour,
high school friends swirling with light,
my husband singular on the green grass,
quiet as an old man.

He moans eating her
last piece of blueberry pie. He's a bachelor,
anything homemade is a feast.
Her meatloaf, scalloped potatoes, chicken noodle soup
swallowed into him, her comforting taste. He takes home
leftovers in plastic containers,
my wife's fingerprints everywhere.

When I woke,
my husband was asleep beside me, blankets untucked,
sprawled across the bed, our awkward bodies.
I bit my tongue to avoid speaking my dream aloud,

his best friend's lips still damp on mine,
the taste of another man's mouth.

                              If she knew
what it means for him to lick his plate clean,
ask for more. Always naive, school girl
innocent with her ponytail, freckles sprigged
across her cheeks. Her nose into cookbooks,
arms full of baby, delicate fingers
fluting the crust of another pie.

                              My fingers
in his mouth, berry-stained lips. Delicious
dream watching him eat at our kitchen table,
each bite full of my hands, the tip of my tongue
tasting its sweetness.

Solomon's Wives, No. 144: Fear of horses

I remember the distinct details as though each belongs
to its own story. The sharp hoof to my chest. The swift
cry of my sister. The servant Milcah scooping me from the sand,
carrying me to the house. The tomato baskets Mother dropped
in the doorway, red fruit rolling down the steps.

Morning and evening, the women wound muslin tightly
around me to hold the broken rib in place, smoothed aloe
into the crescent moon cut below my small nipple.
For seven days they made me lie flat
on the hard cedar bed. Every night, I dreamed
of the black unbridled horse lunging
through the window, its thick mane
stinging my eyes, the sinking bite into my shoulder.

After the bone grew back together, I watched
from the window while the servants watered the horses

under the acacia trees. The women with vessels
on their heads, brought a steady stream
from the well. The men cooled the immense shoulders
and flanks with wet palm leaves.
My sister forever held red slices of melon
to their bare teeth.

When I was 19, his men arrived on horses
with gold for my father and bundles
of fine linen for my mother.
I stayed in the house, refusing to ride
on the jewelled back. Barefoot and dressed
in white silk, I walked beside them all the way
to the palace, three hours over hot sand.

Now, I still watch from the window, the other wives
on a procession of white horses outside the Temple
every Sabbath, riding in long ribbons over the smooth stones.
Solomon on his throne, never counting
to see if one of us is missing, never noticing
in the dark bedroom, the curve of hoofprint
engraved below my breast.

Praise for the Zebra

Because your intentions are so clear,
so black and white.
Because your body speaks in perfect lines,
like licorice strips laid across a horse of snow.
Because you stood too long in the shadows
of the patchwork forest, grew stripes—
half in the shade,

            half out.
Because you are the only animal
worthy of representing the letter Z.

Because I watched you slowly dying
on last Sunday's National Geographic special,
one lion's jaws clamped onto your neck,
the rest of the pride chewing at your withers.
Because you come from the Hebrew *tzebi*,
meaning *splendor* or *beauty*.
Because you are stubborn like me.
Because the sound of your voice, the sharp barking
kwa-ha! *kwa-ha*! carries for miles
over the moonlit African plains.
Because you understand better than anyone
what it's like to live in the prison of your own body.
Because some artists only work in black and white.
Because I am colour blind.
Because my mother's favorite cookies are Dutch zebras.
Because alliteration is inevitable when you are at the zoo.
Because you are painted into crosswalks
on streets all around the world, carry the feet
of pedestrians over seas of concrete.
Because you were the last one on the ark.

Susan Goyette

Susan Goyette, originally from Montreal, now lives in Dartmouth with her family. She is currently working on her first manuscript of poems. Her work has appeared in *The Fiddlehead* and *Poetry Canada*.

I Know Women

The first owl was a girl. Punished for being disobedient, she became the bird
that would never see the sun. I know women like that, part owl. And I know
women

who enter rooms like sunshine and turn everything into mirrors. You've
turned
your mirrors to the wall. You're tired, you say, of seeing yourself. There's
something

to be said of night, of its darkness. You can walk alone with the image you
hold
of yourself and nothing contradicts it. Only then do you feel beautiful.

And in your night of owls, the trees are full of small girls, resting. Waiting.
Their limbs

are pale lavender in the moonlight. This is your punishment; not
  to have become

the owl, but to no longer be the girl. How you loved being her; her arms so
  quick
to dance, her hair grown only for the wind. Now daytime is a
  magnifying glass

in the sun starting small fires of shame all over your body. When did you
  grow so big?
So heavy? You'd give your breasts to be that girl again. And
  though you believe

there's a ceremony for everything, some take so long years can pass
before you realise how much has changed; even you are no longer yourself.

Sisters

We weren't temples or even bungalows. We were apartments. Small
rooms each of us, with no space for storage or sunlight. What was your fire

escape snaked to on those long nights filled with dog whistles
and sirens. What saved you when our hands couldn't reach each other

and our toes stuck to cold metal balconies. When we tried to escape,
the fence gave us splinters and we'd wait for the darning needle to blacken

in the flame, hiding our fingers behind our backs. We had no idea
what else could splinter, what else could break from that childhood

and lodge into us. Now watching our children play in a pool
full of rainwater, we think we are brave, heroically brave to be sitting

here in lawnchairs doing nothing. But this backyard has a secret
path of buried pets and we can name each angel fish, each canary.

Florence

Your bones, the readers of weather, are pressing to your skin
wanting to finally feel the rain.

My daughter's hand curls around my thumb in sleep.
By day she plucks wings from pacing insects, spends them in the wind.

It isn't the flight of ravens I watch, but their claw-sure landing,
bowing branches to the setting sun.

Angels lay their hair across your mouth tonight;
a trap for your last struggling breath.

The night is an apple tree limb,
poised it waits to bend and blossom.

Joelle Hann

Hank Mann

Joelle Hann is a Vancouver-based writer. She won the Lionel Shapiro Award for Creative Writing from McGill University in 1990, and an Explorations Grant for her project "Women and Islands" in 1994. Her work has appeared in *The Fiddlehead*, *CV2*, *Muse Journal*, *Tongue Tied* and *Scrivener*. She is on the editorial board of *Geist* magazine and a contributor to the anthology of essays, *A Feminist Education* (Arsenal Pulp Press). She is currently at work on her first collection of poems, and will be attending New York University to do her Masters in 1996.

To Speak

God's mouth dark on my hair
hope blows around me on the sand.
I am a girl lighting fires near the sea.
Mum's mouth was a window
kept latched, a beach lined
with broken trees.

In my mouth a long sand-stretch
tongue hard like ice and dry.
I am a girl sailing skies, near the sea,
Mum's mouth a porthole,
underwater, an engine room
that seized.

On my fingers a familiar scent.

I am a child playing matches in the dark.
Mum's fingers were a map
in the sea before she pushed off
they promised holier water.

A man's mouth wet on the sky
breathes easy, his hands sailing trees
out from shore, this too
is where I want to go; to go out,
to grow wild with God
to embrace a wilder side
to be the girl who does not tiptoe any more
or offer apology
for waking God with what she knows.

No Cure

Cold night. Frost kills on the ground. Grass
stiffens its shoes. Still stars hang
over us set into the blue. Down at the harbour
trains moan their wheels scraping
to a stop after all the prairie flatlands
and mountain passes. I get into bed.
There is no cure for longing. The trains
are worn out, their black cars empty.
Tomorrow ships will sail
out of port for Russia and Japan. There will be ice
on the roads. Tomorrow all the herbs
in my summer garden will finally be dead.

Black Shirts Drying

Your father's accent hangs above us
like his black shirts soldiering
the laundry line, every last collar-
button shut. On your bed you have
become a boy. I dream I am
your mother and roll my hands over your sleep,
as if to oil it, to turn it between
my legs where they join, secretly
cushioning you, hiding you.
But always in the morning

he's there again, a trellis
of anger up which you grow, crying,
your hair sticking to your face
like leaves, your fingers,
your mouth sucking like a red
hibiscus, a wound. I kiss it, your father
waits to pull your pants
down into his chair. The light goes
dusty in the afternoon. You close me
into your closet, but I hear you and the little
leather crop yelling. the little snake
coming down in a rush, I hear him
part you like a loaf, give your body away.

What can I do, in this closet of fear?
I hang onto brooms and bags
and cry. I call out the numbers of the days
we've had but even this clean bloom
is too small under the endless booming
victory of your father.

Sally Ito

Christopher Smith

Sally Ito was born in Taber, Alberta, but grew up in Edmonton and the Northwest Territories. She has a BFA in Creative Writing from the University of British Columbia and an MA in English from the University of Alberta. She writes short fiction as well as poetry, and her work has been published in *Matrix*, *Grain*, *Dandelion*, and the anthology, *Poets 88*. Her first book of poetry, *Frogs in the Rain Barrel*, was published by Nightwood Editions.

On Translating the Works of Akiko Yosano

To the Akiko who is my mother

It is hard to believe
she is you.

Her hair, wisps of dreams,
spread tangled
on the chest of her poet-lover
is now your sleeping head,
a prayer of darkness,
just before morning.

I rouse you from your sleep
with a long distance call, asking,
"What is 'sasashigeri'? What does it mean?"

And you answer,

"Don't you remember Nanzen Temple
—the way the grass grows there,
lush and thick, like the way your hair
used to trail through my hands,
rustling in impatience with my comb?"

It was as if I had woken you
from your dreaming, my harsh questions
clattering like bamboo sticks
upon the smooth stones of your memory.

You say,

"Translating poetry is impractical."

as if it were impractical
to rouse from your memory, this longing
for my childhood,
and the image of a temple
twenty years past.

('*sasashigeri*' *means thick bamboo grass.*)

Portrait of Snow Country

Brown house-shacks cluster together as
flakes float and settle upon their wooden roofs;
silence in this valley slowly creeps in and moves.
Winter has finally arrived. Snow cold weather.
Black trains pull in, bleating faraway calls,
their billowed smoke fading in to the white air
as more passengers arrive to this 'somewhere'
interior built of nature's shale and limestone walls.
A mountain sketch reveals white sentinel peaks
looming over an old man and his young son,
squatting on their porch, looking into the darkened horizon;

faces flat and dull, colour faded from their cheeks.
A photograph taken, words later scribbled in the corner,
'Father and I on the porch, Winter of '42, New Denver.'

Sansei

i am at my Teacher's house
for my first calligraphy lesson.
Grandmother has given me her old brush
                              and her old inkstone
                              and a blessing
from her faraway Japan lips.

i see the cat
in Teacher's study
for the first time. it is very white and
                         of a pure strain
             of breed
i cannot quite recognize   yet.

it looks at me,   queerly.
i notice a fringe of black
around its paws. upon the desk
is a clutter of rice paper
splattered thick in black
with the inked tracks
of a strolling cat.

'that which prints
its true nature
is what is real,'
Teacher once said.

if that is so, then i know
> the spirit of a Sansei
>> sleeps, still dormant
>>> in the pit of that white belly.

(*Sansei is a third generation Japanese Canadian*.)

Jews in Old China

I

Their history
is without words
in this ancient land.

Who carries the struggle
but the oak, the voices
in the still branches?

II

The silk road
winds around their middles
like sashes of birds in flight .
over the soundless plain.

A ringing bell,
and they are suddenly scattered
pearls in a
wave of blue silk.

III

These sages
cut across pages
of black ink
and rice paper.

Searching, searching.

The fine stroke of the brush,
the black flutter of words,
the sudden rush of wind

and their story is revealed.

Night in Prospector's Valley
Kootenay National Park

we bed early,
the fall of night
heavy as water
on the stone walls
around us.

so dark is it,
we cannot see
the circle of the mountains,
the curve of the glacier,
the pools of water in the meadow,
that flushed before our eyes
at dawn.

it is like a bear,
this darkness—
as if we had bedded in its very fur,
nestling in what we fear most
of this wilderness.

such is the darkness of the mind
before awakening—a shadow, dense and thick,
lumbering upon the grassy slope,

til the snowy edge catches its foot,
and breaks its shape
—a spilled handful of stars
that light the night sky.

Frogs in the Rain Barrel

after collecting, we'd carry them in our hands
      where they became cool pebbles,
still and breathing in the hollow cavern
      of our childish fists.

we'd drop them in the rain barrel
      a small plop,   then,
      the splaying of legs
wriggling in the rippled darkness.

It seemed the rain barrel had no bottom
      just the clear rim of water at its edge,
a pool of still and nether depths
      whose mirrored surface was all.

We thought it an ocean
      for the frogs, we peered over the edge
and watched them swim
      like small shooting stars
bouncing against the rim
      of our reflected faces.

and when they were tired,
      they became still,
their legs and arms outstretched,
            floating,
until their weight collapsed them
      into the palm of our cupped hands.

Joy Kirstin

Joy Kirstin lives in Victoria where she has worked as a writer since returning from two years living in Europe and hitch-hiking through Africa. She was the First Place winner in the League of Canadian Poets 1993 National Poetry Contest.

Grandma in June

Grandma has a heartattack
and I make my first midnight trip
to the hospital where the entire family
gathers in icy green sterility.
We fidget and trace patterns
on the floor, no one knowing how to behave
after years of exasperation at this woman
for whom nothing was enough.

On the bed, her doughy mass heaves up and down,
her toothless mouth, a shrivelled lemon.
Her tongue was the scythe that swung through
every conversation. Even her humour cut us,
jokes about our weight, our jobs, our choices.

No one was out of reach when Grandma
harvested her crop.

The next morning, newly arrived from death
and never one to miss a meal,
Grandma wolfs down the three-course breakfast,
complains the coffee is too weak,
turns and asks me suddenly
if sex is good for me because it never was for her.
The only real question she ever asked me.

After the Pacemaker

In this cold autumn, Grandma cannot cry.
She lives between the worlds, unable
to leave and too tired to stay,
the new pacemaker beating life into her
ninety-one year old body.

I visit two days in a row
the same conversation:
no one cares, no one visits.
Old hurts surround her like feather pillows.
By her bed, a photograph of Grandpa long ago,
the quiet man I barely knew
who used to drink so much that when
my mom was ten and her sister six,
Grandma dragged them to the hospital
where he lay shaking, threatened to leave
because he couldn't even recognize
his only daughters. They say
he never drank again, retreated
to a cloud of pipe smoke. Tobacco was
another world she couldn't enter.

This woman who never got enough
is in my blood, some bruises never heal.
I put on my coat and say goodbye
amidst a litany of all the too-short visits.
There comes a time when everyone must leave.

Summer's Kitchen

Those years we slept a hundred feet apart,
rest and madness roamed the neighbourhood.
Streetlight and sky between us, we wandered
through each other's dreams. Alley cats
crept up and down the road that separated us.

It was the summer your wife left and you fed me.
The sugared kitchen where sourcream
and strawberries spilled over every ending.
One at a time, each dish slid into view,
so many delicacies that some were wasted.
The neighbours feasted on speculation.

In my younger years, I lay with lions in the lilybeds.
Every passion was a sweet anticipation
of the day I would split open, spreading like plum jam.
Later, love required stone and bread.

We didn't speak of the attraction flirting through
our conversations, or the reasons we each had
to never find our way to the same bed. Champagne and cassis,
I sipped my way towards migration, savouring the months
before France beckoned me, spinning tales of Africa
as if I knew her. On your back porch,
we spoke in shadows until dawn.

You led me through the stories of your blood,
the chasms that existed in your body. Black holes

whose imploding truths could suck the light away.
Late night walks down small town streets,
in the twilight we gave birth to stars
and learned to navigate, each of us bound
for nowhere we had been.

It was years before I knew the revolution stored in blood,
the shaking loose of flesh from bone.
Believe me when I say
I never knew the trail of salt I left behind
would lead to you.

Tonja Gunvaldsen Klaassen

Tonja Gunvaldsen Klaassen's work has been published in several Canadian journals, including *Border Crossings*, *Grain*, *NeWest Review*, *Prairie Fire* and *Poetry Canada*. In 1994, she received Honourable Mention in the Bronwen Wallace poetry competition. Coteau Books has published her first book of poetry, *Clay Birds*. She lives in Saskatoon.

My sister's moon through my window

Once, we were remote as the moon, parted
from salt and weedy sea. We watched
the adult world from a darkened bedroom,
safe through the furious night
when our grandmother was pushed
downstairs, falling and falling
and small. A falling star.
From so far away, we wished
for tenderness. We thought everything moved
without change. In the morning,
grandmother would pull thin stockings
over her ankles.

Lifted by night, my sister
was unable to cry. Are you old enough?

he whispered, one hand on her thighs:
the uncle we adored, his mood
a stray dog following him,
not to be touched
because of its hunger. Tenderness is the pull
night has over the ocean,
one blue following another. (Those girls
shouldn't have been in that room, said grandmother.)
At fifteen, I had never seen
the ocean, how great and dark
it could be. Not blue. Silhouetted
in the wan and falling moon, my sister
was invisible.

Eclipse

Hundreds flock to Hawaii to wait for the night
so long in coming, to feel calm
press down on the ocean, hold it
in its bed for seven minutes, the whales
still as air. This one night
people will not walk the beach
looking for coral or white shells,
they will not smell the moonflowers spilling over
tropical nights. They will stand still.
Watching all their reflections disappear
for seven minutes
and never again, not for a hundred and fifty years.

Outside my window the sky dims.
The partial light of a fall moon
is a thin blue shawl once half-draping
the sun, something our teachers told us never to look at.
Blinds pulled down, we watched the moon cross over us

on T.V. We did not hear the birds stop singing or
see the lights blink on Centre Street. Later,
my father turned the yard light off and on
while I stood on the lawn outside.

My father is old. There are things he has meant to say.
One hundred and fifty years is a long time.
I too wait, knowing I have not found all the shells
left behind, I have not finished *Moby Dick*.
I do not know my father's story,
only that he watches alone
on an island
having crossed a line of sleeping whales to get there.

The echo

A *Marabar cave can hear no sound but its own.*
    —E.M. FORSTER, A PASSAGE TO INDIA

She could not have meant to come asking
questions of a cave like *is this love?*
Even with the elephant moving
toward the grey knees of the Marabar
she was not prepared for the unmanageable, the cave
a black bear stretching its throat. Is this love?
In *space things touch, in time*
things part. In darkness, she struck a match,
scratched her name with a fingernail:
its face and the walls' strove to unite
but could not. One *breathes air,*
the other stone. Her mouth
covered by her own hand, the shape of her name
a shadow by the door.

Do we all come with the same breathless question,

leaving ourselves behind
in the search? This is the place I guard, an old grave
so terrible I have no memory of lovers—or hunters.
My father comes to the cave
as though I have called him. He is the shadow,
he rings the bell at the door I can't answer.
I would scratch my name in his bones
if I could breathe stone.
Is *this love*? Maybe
in time things touch. I am a bear
ferocious enough to love anything.

Ice Man

My people built cities of stone
but he can break my heart.
A river traces his name
over familiar places
where even the oldest snow
begins to melt. Cold
is no one's lover. Think of his face
in sun!

A mother would rock him, turn
his balding head in its icy cradle,
carry him home
backwards over rock and time.
I would send him forward
to trade with men he risked his life and lost
in hopes to see.

I am the woman over the rock,
almost afraid of him
—how far he's come!
Carried by waning ice,

he's still wearing the shawl his mother wove
with worried hands. Can I accept
what he has to offer?

What will he ask me
in return?

Fall River

Even the river and falls dried up, and fish
awkward with effort, kept swimming the heat
the day Lizzie's father died. She stood
leaning against a tree like an arm stopped
mid-gesture. Three pears had fallen. Morning
sweeping wide waves of heat, her father
hawking fish again in his last sleep.

He is cold, even in this heat. His hands
now old, still close in tired fists
like those which once hit struggling fish
against stone. Her memory moves water
over fish and fish over falls. He calls
her name in his sleep, painful
feet turning dry and brown. Two pears
lie on the ground.

The third pear, warm in her palm, is bruised
near the end where the white flower dried.
She moves her hand over the fruit,
lifting it like water
to her waiting mouth. The whole morning is
one awful moment when this pear fell
from the tree, its awkwardness
setting it free.

Manitou-night

Manitou is grey
under a mammoth moon, a dark lake
reflecting nothing.
Salt rises in foam,
mimicking the moon.

The water is old. An inland sea
trying to remember
something lost, a sweaty animal pacing.
Far away, the elephants
dizzy with too much grass and sun,
too little salt.

My dreams are made of water,
heavy. I wade through dark.
A herd moves into night, shadows
of elephants returning
from salt caves to savanna.

I've come here alone
(the windows of Danceland boarded up)
trusting the lake
to hold me

afloat. I lick salt from its arms,
alone here
trying to remember
home.

Mama

When the horse picked Mama up by the hair
that time, was she scared?
There is a photograph of her with this horse

in the brown family album. She is standing
beside him, thin in the chilly wind
hands behind her back. When I imagine her
held there, the difference between air and ground
is so small. She was
too close to something I couldn't understand:
the horse's hot breath racing
his long legs still.
(Why didn't he run with her
past the barbed wire and barley fields?)

She used to tell people
I was so much like her, she wanted
to choke me. When she shook my shoulders
or lifted me by the hair
I thought only of my feet leaving the ground,
that small freedom. She doesn't remember
waiting for the horse to run, or for someone
to lift her down. I don't know how
she got away.
Did her mother cut off her hair,
watch thin wisps of it flying in the wind?

Barbara Klar

Barbara Klar's poems have appeared in *Border Crossings*, *Dandelion*, *Prairie Fire* and *Grain*. Her first book, *The Night You Called Me a Shadow* (Coteau), was co-winner of the Gerald Lampert Award. Klar was recently awarded a Saskatchewan Arts Board grant to complete a second manuscript. She has worked as a tree planter in northern Alberta and Saskatchewan for the past eight years. She lives in Ruddell, Saskatchewan with her partner Hal.

The Home

I have taken off my clothes
and I am singing softly
below the blue ear
of the sky. Early evening. Heat
streams from the high field
back to the sun. A doe approaches
the front step where I sing.
Her black nostrils tremble,
eyes wet as stars, long ears
poised like soft antennae.
I watch her
smell me. I lean
against this house at the top
of the prairie, my legs open,

my finger in me
before the whole blue sky

and this slender
four-legged woman
to sing to.

Meadowing

1.
The walking far.
The finding of a resting place.
The body accepts the meadow's verb
and undresses below the sun,
parts the grass, lies down
to the motion of only
mind and breath.
Muscle empties, hollow
as culms of brome grass.

In the hour between
a green field and sky
to meadow is to lie still,
inhale, exhale, rest
in the bluest air.

2.
When the body first pops
into the world, hair grows
from rhizomes below the mother's skin.
Hair, soft as grass, parts to the meadow
outside the birthing hole. The body
rolls onto its belly. Pink skin
dries on the pilrose blades,
more tickle than scratch.

The body laughs its first inhalation
between the earth's legs.

3.
Tall, perennial, dark green grass overflows
the horizon. In the meadow bowl the body
sinks, reaches clay bottom,
a rock growing over.

4.
The body blooms horizontal,
hidden by grass, seen only
by the eyes of clover. Yellow
peers through meadow blades.
The flesh peers back.

5.
Green darners from the nearby pond
mend the air of insects.
In the promiscuous meadow the body
wishes love. Dragonfly wings, wide
as the body, rattle the shoulders
and thighs, land
first on the nipples.

6.
Hands of sun
fold in the meadow's lap.
Hands fold around the body.
The eye of the sun is trusted
enough to sleep under.

7.
The body forgets it was thinking.
The meadow fills the brain
like the brain fills the body.
Meadow wanders the lungs.

Former Sestina For Birds And A Girl

You see across the street a room,
a girl's eyes clouded by cigarette
smoke. Today, you say, she will think
of leaves, her father ready
with the saw. He wants to cut down the tree
that shades the front yard. Its birds

watched her all summer. Small birds
with grey wings just outside her room
in the tangled branches of the maple tree.
You watch her make the bed, light a cigarette
this morning, hear her say she's ready
for winter, time to think

of snow and empty trees. They think
she will always be there, those constant birds,
their feathers still not ready
to go south. With you they watch her room
between the open curtains. Her cigarette
feels warm through the glass, the tree

begins to move. Early fall has stripped the tree.
Its limbs rock in the wind. Her father
hates the girl's cigarette
smoke through the house, the chattering birds
on her brain, the loud music from her room.
He has asked her three times already

today to turn it down. Now he is ready.
To cut down the tree. Burn the wood of the tree,
send the wings and singing from her room.
He says the branches are dead. You think
it might be true. All summer you saw birds
through the spaces where the leaves were gone. Your cigarette

burns a long time, warm as the girl's cigarette.
Behind your window you are ready
this morning to watch her leave. The birds'
nests lean. The brittle tree
sways. Her father paces the yard. You don't think
of stopping him, running out toward her room,

the white twig of the girl's cigarette. Only the birds
fly off. You think as they do that she's ready
for winter, the light the cold leaves by her room.

Planter's Prayer

Mother,
please receive my trees,
grow a decent wage for me.
But please also grow
at least some seedlings in this clear-cut.

Let me pray also
for a dry tent overnight,
shallow mudholes on the road,
good daydreams while I work,
docile bears,
few bugs,
energy and speed,
for the showers to be working,
for a letter from home

but Mother, most of all, for sleep.
I am young and strong but the weariness
upon me could strike down a giant.
Even giants can't plant forests
but I still pray

that you wake me in six hours

with the yellow noise of birds,
coffee and porridge

that I may pick up my shovel
and my hope
and work again.

Evelyn Lau

Evelyn Lau was born in Vancouver in 1971. She is the author of an autobiography, *Runaway: Diary of a Street Kid*, a book of short stories, *Fresh Girls*, and three collections of poetry. Her first novel, *Other Women*, was published by Random House.

Storme

Nineteen

the men file home with flowers in their hands
rubbery petals scent the rain, it is late
the hours pass in dreams, you wake
after the shade of night is tugged down
the men walk past in white trenchcoats, asking directions.
it is February and the flowers in the grocery stores
are dying in their white pails, the grocer is bending down
and picking them up, taking them inside,
taking them away.

the men say they love you, your hair
falls over their alcoholic faces in slick blue curls
you kiss them randomly. oh, the men:
precious as ivory,
dead flowers uprooted in their hands.

all you have to show for this is a few roses,
a smattering of pills in the green glass ashtray,
but he calls you Baby Girl and you watch porn movies together
on the white leather sectional, pop antibiotics and drink scotch
when there's nothing else around.
you know he's your last chance.

he keeps pictures of you in his drawer
your artificial hair whipping against the camera
your model's pout damp with hunger
your eyes like tombstones, black and white.
upstairs the beds are quiet.
at three AM you smash the twisted iron gate and run to the cab
to a driver who assaults you with hard hands
you say nothing, tell no one
is it not enough that you got away?
four AM and you sit in the hallway listening to the rain
emptying out through the drains in the balcony
a stench in the bathroom
knees drawn up in that classic position, you're alive
which should be enough for anybody, but already
you've begun to stop wanting
and more and more men in their ivory skins pass you
in the increasing night, carrying away flowers til all is dark.

Green

and already the leaves have arrived,
my doctor, that blur of green you spoke of four years ago
thickened while you sat, spread in your chair in the sun,
children scuffing bicycles down the alley to the grocery store.
it was not really green, you said, but rather
a haze of green, a fog of green,
a thought of green you could only call light.

I awoke from a dream panicked
thinking I'd missed the arrival of the leaves.
a landlady was taking me from room to room,
each one barren and small and filled
with the sound of typewriters. there was a view
of a beach in the distance, the encroachment of a wave
like a finger, spray hitting the empty shore,
a foreign beach the colour of dust.
the trees were black arms holding up the sky,
crookedly. along the sidewalk in front of the building
that fine mist, that vague rain of green had gone,
and the branches were bent with a new burden of leaves.

four years ago we had word-associated this thought of yours,
this green that wasn't there,
back when mysteries were still abundant
and could be uncovered. yesterday everything was plain
and unbudging as a jug sitting in the sun.
the beach was the colour of your shirt, sand,
the color of your face new to the sun.

in the morning there was no way of telling
if the leaves had come, since there were only buildings,
every room a bleak room. the phone rang loudly
while you, my doctor, went hunting in the park for the hint
of green, the cloud of green you'd held in your mind
for four years, the green that was still mysterious
and therefore solvable, the green that failed to exist.
it breathed along the backs of your thick white hands
as the phone rang in my chest
without a sound, and you groped further and further
down the beach with the voice of the sands.

Eight Months Later: His House

there is a moment of flight in your throat when the key
turns in the lock, and fits
and you follow him inside
a strangled christ dangles on the wall
toy soldiers rally between the bannisters
he keeps a sword beside his empty bed
who is the enemy? how can
the enemy enter and not be frozen
by the blue and white snowflake of this home
a kitchen out of some magazine where kitchens stay
sunny and pine, where the wood is blond
and clusters of dried things smell — herbs, spices, flowers
your pupils spin as if you have stepped
from a black shelter into light
you do not see the three wedding photos on the dresser
where his arm holds a woman who looks happy
even though she is standing in a park by the edge of a cliff
with a good view

Where Did You Learn

In your room overlooking the beach
I stand ringed in black lace bands
the blinds clap above the radiator
salt air and visions of sailboats blow through the window
your hands tear at my hair at my breasts
at so many frustrating buttons
outside the meticulous blinds, the sound of tires on a wet street
swipe of windshield wipers
two or three people walking on the sand

Where did you learn this hate
where did you learn

the sinister suggestion of a belt loosened
the clink of the cold buckle
outside the rains are returning like streetsweepers
the popcorn stands are being closed up
and wheeled away, the water is a grey
plastic sheet broken by concrete islands

Afterwards I want only to be clean
to pump pearly soap out of the container in the bathroom
to tease out underwear from the pile of clothing by the toilet
I want to emerge innocent in a towel and turbaned hair
to walk onto a white iron balcony somewhere
with blue skies, ocean air, orange juice
maybe even a man, waiting against the railing

Father

you fall through a shower of splinters and light
you dance with glass embedded arms
ten feet tall in my dreams, disguised perhaps
but look at how small I have become
in this bathroom stall
beside a man with blood on his elbow
the striped belt of his bathrobe braces my arm
the needle bounces in my flesh
for the first time you leave my thoughts
you who crowd my dreams wearing different bodies
you who walk through doors of glass
and survive
you who fall through skylights
I walk naked through many rooms
you stand cold as a vision
you leave me
I push you through glass doors in my dreams

116

through skylights
my father with the dark face, you appear more handsome
in dreams than in life, I hold up to you the handle
of a child's mirror

The Monks' Song

Once my father heard the monks sing
in a Buddhist temple. At home afterwards
he paced the living room up and down
singing their song
while my sister's bare legs hung over his shoulders
and his hands held her
behind her small tight knees, held her in place.
He was wearing pyjamas that floated through the room
elegantly as any fashionable suit
though they were torn at the thigh, and a flap of cotton hung down
like the skin of a wounded animal.
The monks had misshapen skulls
beneath their shorn hair, they walked round and round
in robes the colour of dark wine
and sunshine in the middle of the day.
Some worshippers carried incense, perfume streaming
from the tips of lighted sticks,
up the stone steps, past the stone lions, inside.
My father took no pictures
though the day was bright as the flash on a camera.
His face was flushed with the autumn heat
as notes from a flute stretched like string
along the corridors, around the circling monks.
I remember their song, he hummed it for days afterwards,
it was one of the last times
his eyes were shiny as bells, ringing
from some region around his heart.

Adult Entertainment

Hot in this apartment
even the paintings sweat
Moulin Rouge with its windmill
silver pillars at the end of a street in Oxford
a charcoal seagull and cloud cover over Paris
in every painting the streets are wider than they are in life
the passerby somewhere between shadow and substance
here the frill of a petticoat
there the skeleton of an umbrella

You live high enough
sometimes the breeze blows off the sea
across the Astroturf on the balcony
and knocks the blinds' plexiglass cord against the window.
I've seen these waterfront streets before
from some other man's balcony
the sulphur pyramids by the dock
the signs on the boxcars
time and temperature blinking from a concrete highrise.

Funny that you can tell me
to lie on your coffee table, paintings on either side of me
women flickering through rainswept streets
the blurred sway of shop signs above doorways
tree trunks bleak as cylinders rising from rock.
the oak table is the length of my body
sticky stocking-tops, slanting breasts
and disobedient nipples, this blur of a body
half-there like the sketched figures hurrying
through European streets on your walls
the edges of their gowns and jackets lifted by the wind
and the painter's brush

In this crisis moment I see all the small things
your mint-green shorts on the cedar floor
my silk shirt in a heap by the bookcase

our dismal reflection in the dark TV screen.
your hand clenches and unclenches
my legs are longer than shadows
the stockings lit with a light sheen
like mist on a windowpane.

I am ready to snap the birch switch
offer you an opened mouth
close my eyes against your oils and watercolours.
let me know when it's over, I will
rise and wash my hands with the jasmine soap in the bathroom
replace sunglasses and lipstick
hail a cab, hang my arm out the window
and laugh
the skies are blue, the money was good
we are lucky to live

Waking in Toronto

nights of green marble lounges and nights
of white bathroom tiles and nights of absence,
hands that try to take you as if you're fifteen again.
your feet are bloody roses of heat
and pain, on the streets
you meet an error of lemon and grape pills.
and the neons of Yonge St. flash the colour of your clothes
while snow falls all around
onto empty university grounds.

and you wake to your life
with feet that have walked the coals of dreams,
the 600 windows of the hotel empty.
at six AM a sun bursts through the shell of cloud
goldening your arms and kneecaps,
igniting the hairs on your calves. and on this bed
are all the unforgotten men.

Michael Londry

Michael Londry is a graduate student in English literature at the University of Alberta, where he has twice been awarded the James Patrick Folinsbee Prize for his poetry. His poems have been broadcast on CBC radio, and have appeared in journals such as *The U.C. Review*, *Other Voices*, *Grain*, and *The Fiddlehead*. He founded and edited the first few issues of *Brave Dalmatian*, a small literary journal, and is currently working on a book-length manuscript of poetry.

Karen Chow

All Canadians Have Wind-Brazen Faces

All Canadians have wind-brazen faces with lots of character.
If you ask sincerely, Canadians will answer any question as best they can.
Most Canadians will not kill a seal unless very hungry and stranded.
Canadian women are more beautiful than the women of any other country in
    the world, except maybe Spain.
Nearly all Canadian dogs are part wolf.
It's hard to take an accurate census of Canadians, because so many are
    essentially nomads.
Canadians choose one mate for life and that's it.
Even at a very early age, Canadian children can build igloos faster than you
    can say them.
All Canadian men can speak French in a way that drives even Frenchwomen
    crazy.

Nearly all Canadians living outside Ontario and Quebec are fluent in at least
    two Inuit dialects.

Educated Canadians prefer Heidegger to Sartre.

Several prominent Canadians were born in canoes.

A Canadian will use a telephone only reluctantly.

All Canadians dream in vivid colour.

Canadians can move clouds with their eyes if they concentrate.

When a Canadian is in love, he or she cannot tell a lie.

A Canadian can survive anywhere in the world if given a jackknife and a few
    bouillon cubes.

Lines for Fortune Cookies

After Frank O'Hara

Tomorrow, you will bump into two people. Though you saw both of them
only yesterday, they will greet you as if you've been missing for years. You
will marry the one whose gaze envelops you like your favourite cashmere
sweater.

Whatever happened to your aspiration to found a new religion?

I love the way you do your hair.

Your arrogance is a symptom of your insecurity. You would do well to admit
this to yourself.

You are like a convertible that is never driven with the top down. Massage
your upper lip. Take long baths. Get drunk much more often.

The person you had a crush on in your adolescence, and who appeared only curt and dismissive towards you, was merely playing "hard to get." This person continues to add to a drawerful of love-letters written to you, but not yet sent.

Your lucky animal is the platypus.

Much can be learned from good comedians. They have suffered and seen. How long has it been since you last woke up with aching cheeks? That's too, too long.

In the late 1960s, a hippie very high on LSD had a vision of you reading this note. Although by now he has forgotten all about you, at the time he wished you all the best.

Tomorrow, someone will swear at you vehemently in a foreign language, and you will not notice.

The man who stopped to help you change your tire three years ago, on Highway 4, still thinks of you fondly every time he sees a bolt wrench.

You have always secretly wished you could have been an orphan raised by a friendly grove of spruce trees. This is good.

Ars Poetica

I would have it that someday my poems are so good that if one of my love poems is overheard at a restaurant, it will have patrons weeping into their soup, will lift all into the perfect sphere of its intimacy.

My domestic poems would have bachelors believing they're married, sitting on the edge of the bed, disoriented for hours.

My kissing poem—even if read silently and alone—may cause the reader's lips to pucker, her body to lean towards an absent lover.

My pimple poems would drive even clear-skinned readers to scrub their faces for days.

My martial arts poems will have readers unconsciously dodging blows, ducking to miss whirlwind roundhouse sidekicks.

My tapioca poem will plunk readers back for a moment into the pudding of childhood.

My later Matisse poems will leave the reader feeling that beautiful blue all afternoon.

My Paul Klee poems will draw one farther into innocence.

My epic poem on the ubiquity of beauty will have readers gawking at the wonders of pavement and of clocks, at the subtle crimsons of apples, the fine symmetry of bridges.

My satyagraha poems will stir riots of protest kisses, bring a little closer the revolution of forgiveness and sanity.

My drowning poems could be read safely only by people of the strongest constitution.

Judy MacInnes Jr.

Born in Prince George in 1970, Judy MacInnes Jr. attended the University of Victoria (BFA) where she received the 1993 Millen Scholarship for Creative Writing. Her poetry and fiction have appeared in CV2, *Geist*, PRISM *International*, Sub-TERRAIN, *The Capilano Review* and *Prairie Fire*. Her short story "nosebleed" won the *Blood & Aphorisms'* fiction contest and appears in the anthology *Eye Wuz Here* (Douglas & McIntyre). She has also published a chapbook with Ga Press, entitled *Super Socco and Other Super Stories*.

Something Round

In grade one, she wanted something she couldn't have. Something to get her hands around, the fur of pubic hair, a muff, a simple protection, a four month pregnancy. She wanted the luxury of travelling eggs before her seventh birthday. She wanted to give birth on the top bunk of Nancy Atamanchuk's bed even before she started menstruating. She wanted something hot to the touch, baby rhinestones, a ticket, a name change, the sensation of a blow-fish expanding in fear.

Surrey Poem

In grade six, Jill started shaving her arms from wrist to elbow with a yellow Bic. I plucked my eyelashes out, mistaking them one by one for eyebrows, hundreds of thin brown crescent moons filled the sink. Jo-Ann dipped Q-tips in Nair and delicately cleaned her nostrils out. Michelle yanked fistfuls from the crown of her head. At the school assembly rules about hair removal were enforced. There were to be no more sleep-overs. Girl Guide meetings were cancelled. Even then, it was never considered safe for girls to be alone in washrooms together.

Pumpfish

When your lover presses his palms and fingers, flat and hard as 2x4s, down on your chest you remember the fish at Link Lake, the summer you were ten and a half. His hands seem to be working on you, trying to revive you like a paramedic would. A few minutes earlier, you were sure he was checking for a pulse. And when he moves from the bed, to the window sill, to the dresser and back to the window sill again, you remember the fish, the lake and also how your father circled the campground, trailer full of daughters, looking for a spot to spend the night. You counted -4-5-6 each time the car, pulling the rented trailer, passed the woodpile 7-8 counts while your cousin, Michael, sat up front between your parents. It was twelve bucks a night for the site he finally picked next to the bathrooms and close to a swing-set your sisters said they were too old to play on. Poplars blocked your family's view of the highway. Your lover comes back to you, stands beside the bed for a moment, covers your legs with the summer bedspread, and for the fifth time tonight he grips the dresser. Your father did his best to circle indoors, too. Pushed himself paper plates, around mosquito coils, buckets of chicken, endless string clotheslines, spinning around the broken zipper of your sleeping bag while your mother rested after a full day of travelling. Now, it's your lover who holds your feet at the end of the bed. After your family had dinner, your sisters, with flashlights in their back pockets, took off down to the lake, leaving you to watch Michael fill the tires of his bicycle. You think your father told you to leave the campsite, find your sisters, urged you to do something other than stare. So you followed your cousin to a different part of Link Lake where certain birds could be mistaken for your older sister's laughter. Your lover is still in the room and waits for you to respond to his mouth, his fingers, his face. His face looking like Michael's when he reached a point in the path where he could see a wooden dock and a boy jigging for fish. An intense face, quick, ready to please. You took the line when the boy was called for supper and jerked on the string as instructed. You imagined your father, underwater, circling the bait. Ready to snap. And tonight you imagine your lover, all fingers, pulling a line. As soon as Michael took over for you, a green and grey fish, with fins as fat as cigarette butts, jumped, hooking itself. You remember the fish dying and gaping, your fingers poking, Michael's hands cupping the fish out of water. You remember him running back to the campsite and placing the damp fish evenly down on a stone the size of a man's hand. You smoothed the fish out while he found a twig near the fire pit, propped the gills open, shoved the bike pump in its mouth, pushed down on the handle.

But on other nights, your lover is like the fish out of water because like a child, like a poem, he starts inside of you. And you push and breathe into his ears and mouth like that bike pump until you hear the sounds of his lips opening, the warm water, the struggle in his voice.

Heather MacLeod

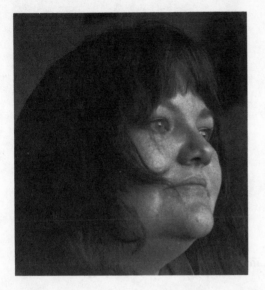

Heather MacLeod is a recent graduate of the Writing program at the University of Victoria. For over three years her life has been divided between Victoria and Yellowknife; she does not have a fixed address. Her poetry has appeared in *Whetstone*, *The Fiddlehead*, *Grain* and PRISM *International*.

Touch the Buffalo

When I left,
my brother came with me,
the only way he knew
to make sure I'd keep coming home.

Leaving—
we made the words we wouldn't
hear in the southern part of our country.
We poured them off our tongues:
Inuit, Inuvialuit, Tuktoyaktuk,
Dene, Dogrib, inukshuk, ulu,
mukluk, Inuktitut, Pangnirtung, Iqaluit.
They dripped off and into the dry
dust of the road from Yellowknife
to Fort Providence.

We saw herds of bison,
we saw muskox and black bears
and Elizabeth drinking beer
in Hay River, her Bronco bent.

The bison followed us out
of the Northwest Territories.
They wanted me to touch them.
At the border, with my brother
asleep in the truck, I did.

I touched the bison,
wanted them to remember me.

When I come home
I greet the bison at the border,
in my mind I say my brother's name,
I say, Buffalo—
I've been gone too long.

My home has been divided
between the Dene and Inuit.
My brother and Elizabeth dance slowly
in the Strange Range their bodies close,
multiplying the distance.

The words and the languages of my home
seem strange on my tongue.
The syllabics of Inuktutuk look only
like odd symmetrical shapes.

An elder tells me I should chew
on the dirt. I should run my tongue
over my land.

Strawberry

for my brother, Kevin MacLeod

I

We were born without maps.
So how can we be expected
to figure out where we are supposed to be?
Our mother apologized to us
in 1985, said she was sorry
for having brought us into the world.
She sat on the kitchen chair, a scrub brush
in her left hand
and she was crying.
I said nothing; neither did my brother.
Instead we washed the floor,
what else could we do?

Later we went strawberry hunting,
finding small, blood red buds, juicy to eat
but tart on the tongue.
When our mother ate them, she forgot about
the badness of the world, she forgot,
but we remembered
the sweet, tart goodness of strawberries.

II

The summers we spent as children
were taken up by Meadow Lake,
absorbed by the water, the sand,
the rocky quarters;
we learned how to live at the lake,
close to plants and animals,
close to each other.
My brother discovered the bird

that pretended her wing was broken.
He wasn't fooled by her act
and found her nest.
We hunched over
as he held one of her small,
oval, cream-coloured, spotted eggs
in his right hand.
He broke it gingerly, spilling
what was inside, so we could look at it.
I didn't like it.

In the tent he brought me strawberries
to take away the bitter taste.
We fell asleep beside one another,
strawberries in the middle.
I woke because I could feel something
moving in my hair,
it crawled across my head, down my arm,
moving through my fingers onto my brother's stomach.
It was small, a little, green lizard.
It curled up and slept in the hollow
of his belly button and I watched them sleep.

III

We travel without maps, my brother and I,
we move around the country without direction,
we follow the feel of the road,
ignoring the signs that will only lead
us in the wrong direction.
He lives in the north on the south side
of Great Slave Lake—

somewhere he is eating strawberries,
lying in the hot sun; tiny, green lizards
moving in and out of his belly button.

Reflection

She comes from all the blood,
made from all the secrets,
she buries the truth, tries to hide it from me.
Does she remember
what she's done with it?
Where did she put the things
that really happened?

Late at night I steal the truth from her.
It's precious, I tuck it into the corners
of the room and under the covers.
Late at night I tape my legs together,
wind the tape from hip to ankle,
but she parts them when I'm not looking.

I get up from her body, and gather the truth
from the corners.
I pull out my birth certificate,
trace my name and my birthdate.
Smell the paper,
lick the name of the city
I was born in.
I cut my father out,
cut my father's name out—
large hole in this paper,
large hole.

Barbara Nickel

Barbara Nickel grew up in Rosthern, Saskatchewan and now lives in Vancouver. She is co-winner of *The Malahat Review* 1995 Long Poem Prize, and her work has appeared, or is forthcoming, in many publications including *Grain*, *The Fiddlehead*, *Poetry Canada* and *Prairie Schooner*.

Twin Sisters to be Presented to Society *

I found them in a box in Government Publications: labeled,
pressed flat in microfilm, wrapped around a plastic spool. I
threaded them in and New York, 1931 hummed by: auctions, rooms
with running water for $2.50—and the twins' faces like two
white moons, stones I might hold cool against my cheek on a muggy
afternoon. The Misses Marion Carol and Gladys Muriel, just
sixteen, summer offerings of pure skin and hair, well-bred
virgins. Was the bidding for two, together, identical pleasure?
The Yacht Club in evening light, the stockbrokers, lawyers. Who
was the winner, in the end, who laced their waists, bit their
soft lips?

headline from the New York Times, *July 21, 1931*

Marion, 1936: To my Twin Sister

The Hudson River, where we used to fish
in freckled rushes damp against our skirts,
where water like a silk scarf wound a hush
around our aching chatter, smothered hurt.
I fashioned our escapes. We slid from naps
unnoticed to the wood and narrow path;
the junipers whose crusty tears of sap
embodied us, small dregs of Father's wrath.
I picked a hook. You fastened it.
We clasped our hands and cast for rainbow trout.
You hauled one in—I raised the stick and hit
its judging eye, like Father's, shot with soot.
We battered it a hundred times in mud;
our petticoats all sullied with its blood.

Marion, 1939: To my Twin Sister

Remember Mother's voice, the way it fussed
about our teagowns, pinning words: *soft, please*
and *grace*, like charms whispered into our tucks,
trying to cloak our awkwardness with ease?
She didn't cover Father half as well.
Late nights we heard him stumble in the door
and sing and roar for her; his rants would swell
like breakers dashed against his yacht. She bore
each lashing with the hush her family name
had taught. We picked at lint. We saw the years
engulf her in the rooms. Her voice became
a tick, a wash of silk. She disappeared.
Today I heard the clock's insistent chant:
Tell Gladys she should leave before she can't.

Gladys, 1940: To my Twin Sister

I dreamt us back inside our mother's womb,
our veins arranged like doilies of point lace
around each heart, each tiny, poppy moon.
Your toes, like drops of rain against my face
tapped messages—*begin*—*swim to the light*.
Somewhere an anchor lifted. Waves collapsed
and sucked us down a whorl of pain as tight
as corsets, skin on skin, our fingers clasped.
Tonight the desert of my husband's back.
My vows are dust motes, years of threadbare lies
collected on my packed valise, the cracked
remains of mother's vase. I run outside.
A maze of streets shellacked with grimy ice,
my train squeezing through tunnels to your face.

Kevin Paul

Kevin Paul— "A very long time ago, the survivors of a great flood named their homeland W̱SÁ,NEĆ and themselves the W̱SÁ,NEĆ people and we are still here. I am a W̱SÁ,NEĆ Indian. We live on the Saanich Peninsula on the southern tip of Vancouver Island."

Ceremony

A crow walks
its muddy,
kneeless walk
across
a freshly plowed field.

In this light,
I see the crow
as crows are—

so much seems possible.

A Pheasant on Deer Mountain

It is early spring and morning,
before the sun has arrived.
There is just enough light
to mark the path: A shadow,
darker than the twisted trees
guiding it into morning. She is
little more than silhouette
when she steps one step   then another
from behind an arbutus tree
into the wet path.

There is just enough light
that she can see
I am a man and not a bird.

Because she has no words
and I have no song, she accepts,
and I settle for a safe distance between us.
She was designed to disappear,
if she hid
I would pretend not to see her.
She stays on the path ahead of me
and we stop three times
before we reach the top of the hill:

We stop in a clearing
and have a look at each other;

I wait, while she has a drink from the creek;

We stop once to listen.

I have come as far as I am able
when we reach the top of the hill.
I hear her leave:

136

the sound of her disappearance,
the sound of her soft body
beating into the morning air.

The sound of a stone
and the stone's echo,
rolling down the granite hill:

The idea of me standing on the edge
of the small valley
while she lands in the meadow below.

Belly Button

My mother was careful
about what she ate
when it was my turn

inside her. It was already me
well before she had problems
getting up out of chairs.
Already me before I had elbows
to poke her with,
her hand on her tight skin
waiting for my next move.

It was my presence in her,
my nearly unstoppable growing,
that made her breasts tender,
her tail bone sore,
made her hungry and ill.

So many times
she has spelled out the odds
I was up against.

Her joke about my arrival,
the pill in my tiny fist.

When I was old enough to be
curious, I asked her
about the small round hole in my tummy.
She said, "That's your belly button,
it used to be your mouth."

A Fish on Pandora Street

The Indian man leans in the archway.
The red door behind him opens
to his pocket of night,
to the odd mood of night
kept there in mid-afternoon.
The slow blues is released
from the tavern
then closed-in and gone.

The man, with his round mouth,
is smoking. His sad day dream
is there while he sucks at the cigarette,
tastes it, and blows the smoke into the walkway;
brown tobacco evaporated

into white smoke. His true form
is only known when he walks away
and the smoke from his cigarette
moves in an eddy of air around him.
It is as though someone could take him
out of that air
and he would not know
what went wrong.

Still Falling

Below the burial ground, _KENNES
has taken to its winter form,
the echo of its rhythm stumbling
hard into this ceremony of grief.

    "_KENNES" is the name of the stream
    and the name of the whale
    that died in the mouth.
    I say the word and I can see
    the whale that beached itself there
    and the ancient man who found it;
    the fresh water of the stream
    falling around this enormous, slow-
    breathing creature;
    the whale feeling
    its own weight
    for the first time.
    I am standing with the man just briefly
    as he says "_KENNES" and looks into the waterfall,
    then at the whale
    washed up on the shore at low tide.

The winter has always been hard on us.

But when a family stands here together,
we know just what family is—
look how we hold on to each other
as we see the casket sink into the ground,
my uncle's body
inside. All of us hold a corner of this story,
though some of us have no hands
to speak of.

It's true,
when I feel helpless

I am the only one
who feels this grief:

    "KENNES" is the name of the stream
    and the name of the whale
    that died in the mouth.
    I say the word and I can see
    the whale that beached itself there
    and the ancient man who found it;
    the fresh water of the stream
    falling around this enormous, slow-
    breathing creature;
    the whale feeling
    its own weight
    for the first time.

How long had whales returned here
before this one? How long have people
come to witness their return?
To see them chase the young salmon
into the small bay
nearly to the foot of the falls.

The body of a whale is like any body,
the canoe for an ancient spirit. The water,
like time, moving to the same edge for so long.

Still,

I feel as though I am witnessing the first
whale to wash ashore here:
My father's last living brother.

Uncle,
our last handshake in Saanich,
this shovel full of dark earth
on your grave.

Michael Redhill

Michael Redhill lives and works in Toronto. His books of poetry include *Impromptu Feats of Balance* (Wolsak and Wynn) and *Lake Nora Arms* (Coach House Press). He has two books forthcoming: a poetry collection, *Asphodel*, and a novel, *Martin Sloane*.

The Return

Lake Nora has gone missing in her own body.
Submerged trees leave question marks
swirling in the water. From our canoe
we see filaments of decay hanging up
and the sun moving through them unchanged.
You call out your own name
and the shale walls send it back incomplete
as if woken from a dream. The quiet scares us—
we feel the loss of something unnamed,
like someone has sealed off the world below us.
I'm watching you, you're watching me.
It feels like one of us might disappear,
suddenly. Then something
leaves a rock and enters the lake—

all we can see is the echo spreading.
It comes out to touch the boat. *Stay with me.*

Deck Building

The long summer it went up
nail by nail—difficult
to reconstruct. The once huge days
clench into hours of the mind,
the pictures splintered, moving
tongue and groove into each other.
Here, a hammock and a line of berries
budding. Here, a mother
rescuing cold children from a lake
into towels, rubbing heat
into their bellies. I see my
purpled fingers in her hand,
her breath warming them.

Those summers the cottage grew
in increments like our bodies.
New shingles, stripped wood,
front room, a deck. My father and I
built it from pine and cedar.
The sap glued our hands to the wood.
His back when he worked
was spotted with pearls.
Beer nearby, its salty edge
on my tongue. I'm twelve,
big enough to share a beer.
As we hammer and fit
the dogs chase squirrels. Beautiful
dogs, prisoners of summer.
I feel the hammer blows

up my arms, the satisfying
force that slides the nail in,
its narrow sound.
We create a false earth. Flat
as the sky looks, knocking each plank
into place, lining them up
like bean rows. The imagined
night-drinkers appear
as ghosts in my mind. I see them
walking on the pieces
we put together.

By the end of the summer, we were
staining it, and when it was finished
he stood out on it, alone with his thoughts,
still, like a tree. I watched him
from the window, seeing how he saw
his world grow up around him
and although I could feel his thoughts
I didn't know what they were.

Phases

Ich glaube an Nächte

Watching the garden winter under the moon,
we think of the brown animals
under the earth. Or the bulbs
of the jonquils frozen there
with their orange eyes clenched in coils.
White and silent night, the air cold as iron
and the lake like an old woman under a blanket.
We gave your grandma marijuana tea
to lull the cancer clenched in her like fists.

Our legs are weak after making love
but we walk across the solid lake.
We're wrapped in the husk of a Bay blanket,
the air smells like wool and our heat
billows around us, animal. The lake
clicks as we walk, a photograph
curling up at the edges. Far under,
hibernating fish drift in the current,
their bodies curving back and forth,
while above them the moon
glows on the snowless patches—
a white heart expanding under the ice.
And in our blanket, our bodies
hold the shapes of the people
whose cells we slept in for generations.

Happy Hour

The chicken magnates sit
by the fireplace, spouting prices
in clipped dactyls, cigars glowing
like stars in the corner of the room.
Their wives circle the buffet,
loading up plates for them. Dogs
and children crowd underfoot, the din
is enormous. Outside,
incessant rain. Lake Nora is transfigured:
goose-flesh. All day my mother has prepared
for the gathering, poppy bagels, withered fish
with the eyes still in, a huge
anniversary cake.

Later, the grandparents stand
at the edge of the candles, chins glowing

and blow them out. A camera
grinds in someone's hands sucking up
the moment, freezing it in camera amber.
People navigate the thin hallway
to the bathroom, flat against the walls
like spies. A punch-line floats in the air
how should I know—I'm fourteen miles from home!
and my mother turns, laughing,
her mouth full of cake.

I look around. The chicken men are drunk,
their empty glasses tilt on their bellies.
A child has fallen asleep. A woman
I have never met thumbs up poppy seeds
from the table and eats them as she argues
with her neighbour. The crazy
aunt and uncle who still love each other
kiss in a corner. After this is all forgotten
we'll long for the background
where the unnamed visitor appears
in all the films, whose name
no one remembers. We'll watch those films
years from now, reviewing
the divorced and the dead,
that old ambient weather.
Someone will say, I wish I could go back
and someone else, No, never.

Indian summer

Summer, with its smooth body
recurs like a dream. It has
the beautiful energy of women.
During our first winter

it never stopped snowing.
Its shadow fell across our faces.

As I sometimes go mad
for the love I miss, so everything
must reach back. The indian summer
is pity, gone love returning
its music far off, but remembered
as all our pasts, as certain
as drinking water.

Like the space made
between first finger and thumb
we can bring it back
over and over. So we recall
the scent, the sense
of the space we loved in,
grew warm in, disappeared from.

There is little difference
in the shape of a hand
against your face, and the same hand
empty.

Reconciliation

For two hours they've argued, their language strange,
their predicament familiar. The late-hour
tea-drinkers, silent at their tables, have taken sides. He's
vivid, his hands holding her in his angry
atmosphere, yet
I want him to win, want her to take him back as bad
as the café's women want to move to the young girl,
their bodies bent into her as if she were light.
She's dressed in black, steadied at the table

with her hands splayed, her back taut, her legs
braced under the table as if for aftershocks. To his
pleas—so busy-mouthed, so darting-eyed—she offers
birdlike demurrals. I glance up at a woman sitting alone,
but can't pledge love, turn my light down again. His
fingertips are leaving white aureoles on her arm. How long
before she breaks? Her head goes down and her shoulders shake,
he puts his hand in her black hair. Mi *corazon* she says
and kisses him over the empty plates.
I can see her eyes behind her shaking lids
the pupils so nervous and sexual under
the pale skin and I feel as if I am watching her sleep,
seeing her face in the deepest part of the night
when your lover dreams and you cannot wake her.

Jay Ruzesky

Jay Ruzesky has lived in many parts of Canada, and currently resides in Victoria, BC. His books include *What Was Left Of James Dean* (Outlaw Editions), *Am I Glad To See You* (Thistledown) and *Painting The Yellow House Blue* (Anansi). He teaches at Malaspina University-College.

Sergei Krikalev on the Space Station Mir

> this is for those people
> that hover and hover
> and die in the ether peripheries
> —MICHAEL ONDAATJE, "WHITE DWARFS"

My name is Sergei and
my body is a balloon.
I want to come down. I
tie myself to things.

My eyes try to describe your
face, they have forgotten.
My ears echo your voice.

I am a star, you can
see me skating on

the dome of night. My blades
catch sun from
the other side of earth.

Days last an hour and a half.
No one else lives here.
My country has disappeared,
I do not know where home is.

I am a painter standing back.
I watch clouds heave like cream
spilled in tea, I see
the burning parrot feathers
of the Amazon forests,
ranges of mountains are
scales along the hide
of the planet, the oceans
are my only sky.

This is my refuge. There is
no one else near me.
Do you understand what that means?

Elena, I am
cold up here.
I hang over Moscow and
imagine you in our flat
feeding little Olga
in a messy chair.
When I drift out of signal range
I do things you
don't want to hear about.

These feet do not know
my weight. A slow
balloon bounces off the walls.
I do not feel like I am flying.

I want to come back and
swim in your hair.
I want to smell you.
I want to arrive in the world
and know my place.
Think of me. I am yours adrift.

Let me describe
my universe: I can see for years.

Night of the Skagit County Parade

in your most frail gesture are things which enclose me,
or which i cannot touch because they are too near
your slightest look easily will unclose me
though i have closed myself as fingers.

—e.e. cummings

I want to say something
thoughtful about the weather. My body
is a medieval village and the wind
is blowing through it.
What right does the air have
to set this free?
But your fingers on my back tracing
the blades of my shoulder
nullify the draught's breath because lightly
in your most frail gesture are things which enclose me.

At four-thirty a.m. here
in the valley of eternal spring
you shift to the other side of the bed.
Your hand shuts and loosens.
Under the sheet's white page
we are paper dolls who tear

150

easily apart at fragile places:
our hands, cold-touching feet.
There are the blossoms of your body whose absence I fear
or which I cannot touch because they are too near.

Our own desire we recognize. To be desired
is something else. I thought you were
similar in this way: others' desire,
pardon the pun, is what we want.
In the afternoon you dug in the garden,
bent into the earth, your knees
leaving imprints of you there. I would not let myself soundlessly
kiss the sweat from your red shoulder.
But I stared, hoping you might turn and see
your slightest look easily will unclose me.

Now is the morning of the flower festival parade in
Skagit County, Washington. In an airplane hangar
luminescent floats look naked because cold has closed
the daffodils and irises that are their skin. Every
band member in red suede cowboy boots, all
baton twirlers, parade clowns, cheerleaders, and singers
are opening tens of thousands of petals with their sighs.
Miles away we are blossoms curled inward from the cold,
and the idea of you opened by breath lingers
though I have closed myself as fingers.

Crocuses

blooming under the trees, even
the beginnings of daffodils, tulips, the sun
arching a little higher: a bright kid
getting better at back handsprings, there were buds
on the branches I carved off with
a Japanese pruning saw, the shining

blade. And a glass cover over all of it that isolated me
from anything human, there was the phone
angry as a parent's voice calling
a late someone home for dinner, and him—
small malevolent god crouched
above the jar—how long it would take
the bug to suffocate?

> "My greatest crime is the curiosity
> that disturbed the progress of a snail."

There were the words of the Chinese poet. Me
dousing the pile of prunings
with gasoline, the sparked
match and all the times I treated you
with less reverence than you
deserved, though what was lacking in those moments
was a lack in me too, there was my blaming
you anyway, and always the desire on my part
to hear in your voice the passion we left
behind somewhere. There were flames,
and spiders escaping, their world
heating up, and next door the two girls who ran
about the yard catching ash on their tongues.

Single Mother's Garage Sale

This is a fear I cannot know.
I am looking at a woman
who studies me
from outside the elevator.

Earlier, maybe, in an
afternoon's back alley,
she is moving through

the shadows, past
green garbage bags leaking
grass clippings, past remnant
bits of car repairs, she is
walking toward the gauntlet's
end when a man appears
bypassing without acknowledgement like
a car on a Saskatchewan highway.

Then she is milling among others
on someone else's well groomed
lawn looking over tables of stuff.
She picks up what looks
like a cigarette case
but is a pair of binoculars.
The afternoon becomes surreal.
She turns them on
the house and it looks
like a nice house,
the sun blinks through
bits of the stucco's glass.
She can see the label on a
coffee pot; Melitta, sounds
Spanish when she says it.
A stack of children's books
leans dangerously. Mostly,
there are piles of small
textile arms and bodies, empty sweaters.
She is admiring the garden,
strays off to study
camellia blossoms white as teacups.
Alone again she dreads the thought of
someone grabbing her from behind,
the acute distance between the
knife-edge and her throat,

raw places on her heels from
being dragged behind the
building, anticipates a bruise
on her lower back from cement,
red-black places around
her mouth and eyes where
he might stifle her with
snake-thick gloves.

She returns to the cluttered yard
sees a friend, sees several
friends around the coffee urn.
One of them drives her home
and stays on the street
until she is safely
inside the apartment. She
waits for the elevator,
its doors open to expose
a man looking at her.
She hesitates, steps in.

Roller Coaster

My father laughed and it was
the first and only time so far
I've heard him do it; a real
laugh deep from inside
climbing like an artillery shell
up his throat and pushing out of
his Edvard Munch mouth.
We were commuters aimed at heaven,
riding a steep, open train toward
the sun god at the end
of the line, padded straps

reefing our shoulders against
plastic seats. This was
the last place I wanted to be,
locked in like an astronaut,
someone else driving,
lunch rising in my chest.
My eyes were open to
the whine of pulleys as we
ascended a slope snow wouldn't
hold to if snow fell through the
ridiculous summer air. There was
a moment as we reached
the first peak and crested
when I smiled too at weightlessness,
the feeling as you float
from a swell in a fast highway until
most of me dropped. I felt
my stomach's desire
to stay behind up there where it could see
halfway to Saskatchewan and
to bail out again at
the bottom as we were
caught like eggs by a
giant hand and sent up again
over a short rise only to
plunge face-first at the ground
continuing as we rolled
through a giant loop, swooped
with the energy of descent and
twisted through a series
of corkscrew turns, our
brains in startled mobius,
my father wide with giddy terror.
Somewhere along the way he

reached over and squeezed my hand
and our astounded spirits
or some other part of us
that it seemed we could do without
for a while raced behind
like afterimages as we rolled on
through the inverted morning,
clutching each other,
wearing death-masks of happiness.

Gregory Scofield

Gregory Scofield is a Métis poet, dramatist and nonfiction writer who was born in BC and raised in northern Manitoba, northern Saskatchewan and the Yukon. He is currently living in Vancouver and has had two radio dramas produced by the CBC. His first book, *The Gathering: Stones For The Medicine Wheel* (Polestar Press) won the 1994 BC Book Prize Poetry Award. His latest book is *Native Canadiana: Poems From The Urban Rez* (Polestar Press).

Call Me Brother

"You never know when you're talking to an Indian," he
says wisely because I am only half which we both know
is not the real issue but the way I look which makes it
next to impossible not to spot me sticking out at a
powwow because I have the tourist look that offends
my darker relations who don't see me as related but a
wannabe muzzling up around the drum to sing 49ers
except I feel the beat like my own heart racing when
curious eyes study if I am just mouthing the words or
actually belting them out because I am a true die-hard
Skin with blue eyes that really screws up the whole
history book image except my roots can't be traced to
the Bering Strait but nine months after European
contact which to this day hasn't been forgiven even
tho we all have some distant grandpa who at one time

or another took an Indian wife which we tend to forget
because anything but pure is less than perfect and we
all secretly need someone to be better than so the
next time you see me up dancing call me brother

Talking Because I Have To

When first I saw rye whisky
get the worst of him
he was smashing everyone in sight.
Hearing my mother scream, I ran downstairs.
My kiddy voice was no match.
She just lay there, convulsing under his
boots.

My mouth still knows what happened:
puffed-up lips I remember.
The rest is hazy, a long-ago movie. Someone
yells, "Go to the neighbours, call the cops."
And it ends there

Leaving a disturbed feeling over the years.
Even now, they say, "Greg, forget it."
Going on is made easier because they won't
talk. I talk because I have to.

That Squawman Went Free

On the street   it had been leaked
by the looks of her
he'd slapped her around
enough damn times
to make himself feel better
how he couldn't get a real woman—
a whitewoman to hop

Every week his mouth

plastered to her tits
those fat stub fingers
dug in her spoon
craving a shrivelled dick cure
he even made her suck
the useless gut   and blamed her

The money went up her nose or
in her arms—when the veins collapsed
she used her legs
her skid sister said
sometimes he had the decency
to wait until the bruises healed
before he picked her up again

Last month her body was discovered
by the railroad tracks—they figured
another Native suicide/overdose
but there was some talk
about a bad date
someone reported his licence plate number—
all we heard was
     Welfare flew her home

Wrong Image

for Gareth Kirkby

Their necks were stiff from watching
Indians downtown
who'd piss in the back alley
at closing time.
From their cars they were safe,
those honkies.
We knew they were there, sulking around
like a weak species
trying to build themselves up.

In high school
Emma & me were the only Indians.
We started hanging out together, formed
the very first least likely to succeed club.
None of those white kids
could down a mickey of rye like us.
We didn't even need a mixer.
We'd just pop off the cap
and chug-a-lug.

Sometimes they'd stand out on the street
straining to hear our drunk talk.
We spoked pretty broken
so when dey mimicked our dalk
it was authentic not Hollywood.
They joked about our appearance,
said we shopped at Sally Ann.
Once we overheard them laughing
and chased them through the skids.

In the school library where I thought
and brooded a long time
I crouched over history books
staring sullen at those stoical faces.
Me & Emma got names too.
I was her chief and she my squaw—
though to our faces they wouldn't dare
for fear of an Indian attack.
Me & Emma just smiled stupid.

Last summer I spent the afternoon with a journalist.
I wore linen and leather sandals, spoke of
racism & class & why I began writing.
The interview was about survival and healing.
In the article I read he was disturbed by
the predominance of alcohol in my work—
how I perpetuated the negative image of Native people.

After ranting & raving & screaming at the appropriate sources
I smiled stupid, and wondered what ever became of Emma.

Kohkum's Lullaby

Kiya mato noosisim
Kiya mato
Kiya mato

Kosim'mow nichimoose
Kosim'mow
Kosim'mow

Tome'pah noosisim
Tome'pah
Tome'pah

Sakehi'tin nichimoose
Sakehi'tin
Sakehi'tin

———————————

Don't cry grandchild
Don't cry
Don't cry

Lay down sweetheart
Lay down
Lay down

Go to sleep grandchild
Go to sleep
Go to sleep

I love you sweetheart
I love you
I love you

Nadine Shelly

Nadine Shelly was born in Papua, New Guinea, grew up in northern Saskatchewan and now lives on Saltspring Island and in Vancouver. In 1990 she published her first book of poetry, *Barebacked With Rain* (Exile Editions) and received a protégé award from Morley Callaghan as part of the Toronto Arts Awards. She has had work published in *Grain*, *Exile* and *The Capilano Review*, and is currently completing work on a second collection of poetry.

A Preoccupation With Bridges

this ceremony is small

small as a pore on your skin
small as a child in the sun
small as a bud on the tongue, sweet rosebud of tongue,
small as the dip of a spoon
     into a silver dish
an eggcup, perhaps.
Yes, this ceremony is small.

I have made it this way
out of great need
to reduce things to a size
so much less than myself.
I have torn paper into

pieces a thousand times smaller
than anger, ripped from my hands.

it is the crossing of the fingers,
the crossing of the heart.
I am the smallest word I know,
you are three times larger, at least.
What is the smallest thing you said to me?
No. You said no
and it reduced me to my simplest terms.
Love over and over; divisibility
on a downward slope.

less than this is nothing.
this ceremony is small as nothing.

Because my breast is where the fairest doves rest

for jessica

my beautiful mutilator;
I, with scabs on my knees
and sticks in my hair,
I am no rival.
But my love is like the sky
and is not diminished.
Your beauty wounds me,
my body has a thousand bleeding mouths.
I would kiss you with them all.

The Sun Has Bones

for brian and louise

in mayan temples
goddesses carried
people's souls in
small pouches hung
about their necks.
the souls were small bright
stones, as children
this is what we knew.

every morning they
would dance, shape
their bodies into
absolutions for the
gathered masses.
later they might
languish in the heat
the sky so large
it would nearly crush them.
at these times, their voices
became tiny, the sound
of beetles in the grass.

nights we watched them fly
their faces webbed in
adoration, bonfires
marking patterns of
the sun.

deep inside
your soul might rattle

ravenous

behind the blind hood of the moon
moans the one broken, black bird
with no sound. Blinking

a single soft eye at the sky
you see her vision
in the blink of an eye

she is hiding her hunger
under her tongue, keeping
the quiet in a stone or a drop

of red blood upon a black rock.
Black bird, black rock
red drop in your eye

veins in her blue eyes
are branches that seek the blue sky
blue eye blue sky

stretching along wet limbs
to an open mouth, a raven's
red tongue

to become
to be born without sound
above a shy field, silver wet

glint of the sky. Her cry
like a knife, like a slip
of the tongue, quick flick

of the wrist, blood drops
to the rock to arise like a flock
of redwings, the silence she sings.

Waiting in the River Valley

Waiting in the River Valley

horizons are high
in the silence of death
words lie blackened and used
by our feet
cinders of remembrance

the sky is blank
bright without sun
we are searching
for a focus

back and forth back and forth
in red sand
my leg is a metronome
counting out our grief

without change time is irrelevant
we have decided to wait
for the rain

Long Beach

shrank back
she shelled
herself into a shrimp
sized thing; small
silk husk of hair
grown to hide her eyes,
catch her finely,
in part. Parts of her

were poking through;
bones or small buds,
birdlike things.

she appeared one day
on the shoreline
washed out, washed in,
she was pale.
a man thought she had drowned,
blew air between her
lips, she coughed up pearls
and slippery black eels. The man
was afraid and left
without his footprints or his name.
The girl kept both
and was amused, she wore them
on her body
soft sloped as the sea.

Karen Solie

Karen Solie was born in Moose Jaw in 1966, and raised on the family farm in southwest Saskatchewan, near the small farming community of Richmound. She moved to Victoria in 1993 to take her MA in English at the University of Victoria, and is beginning her PhD at UVic this fall.

Staying Awake

I

It's agreed.
Fall is the time for it.
Harvest done,
insurance paid up.

This is the third in as many years
and how curiously, neighbours say,
each in his own way.

The first hung himself in the barn
seeking comfort, we suppose,
in the rising smell of hay
the warmth of his horses.

The second,
hands around wrenches in his pockets,
drowned in the dugout in back of the house
among trout stocked in spring.

But this last,
so violent.
Nothing romantic about a shotgun in the mouth.

> Young guys crowd around the truck
> towed from his yard into town.
> Is *that blood*? Is *it*?
> Just *dirt*?
> Is *this bone or glass*?

In time this death too becomes a cliché,
like the way his living body fit
into hollows of the land,
how his vision curved with the fenceline.

Air, water, and finally blood.
We imagine it
crawling and soaking into earth
he'd worked since he was a boy.

II

The wives don't talk amongst themselves,
each believing her man's mood
a secret between them.
Those days,
sometimes a week after such a death,

they move in heavy silence with him
as quiet grain moves.
And while the empty prairie sky is filled
with clouds of its men sleeping,
each woman, unheard, hides ammunition

in jewelry boxes and underwear drawers,
her nights all the darker for being awake.

Toad

I am a seed, a world inside
a tough weathered wrinkling
of vegetable green.
Insoluble in liquid space
of anger, fear, love
or other human acids
I sit on the bottom like a stone. Shifting
only slightly with tremor
or violent wave,
I ride out the winters.

But do not mistake
the stillness of my living for cold.
I am warmed enough in my smallness,
in my wet and quiet,
so as not to be judged
by warm-blooded standards.

Invisibility is my loveliness.
In assuming the posture of water or air
I am reclaimed, while you,
large and cold and sinking on your shores,
can only hear my voice, my beauty
through the air.
Just listen.
Even when I cry for you
it sounds like singing.

Dry Mother

Little brother, seeing
that blind wall approach,
his tricycle flipped end over end,
asks if it's the end of the world.

We who live
here in the lap of this dry mother
know from our beginning that it will come in dust.
Have heard those drifts
that trouble the fenceline in daylight
wash around the house after dark
in a way that reminds of how a good rain sounds
like the suck and hiss of fire.
Mornings, we've seen perennials dead
even on the lee side and have feared
the loss of each other to shrouds
of our own land spun
by wind that will not stop.

But it does this time, as before.
Another calm apology
for seed planted in door frames,
these newly hatched sparrows
choked by earth
that leapt up to bury them.

Carmine Starnino

Carmine Starnino's poems have appeared in *Quarry*, *Poetry Canada Review*, *The Antigonish Review*, *The Fiddlehead*, *The Malahat Review*, *The Urban Wanderer's Reader*, *Vintage '93* and *Cyphers* (Ireland). He lives and writes in Montreal.

Picking the Last Tomatoes with my Uncle

As if unearthed, they gave off the smell of damp loam;
a thick musk, like smoke, that made my eyes water
as we knelt together, our heads bent, and emptied
the plastic basins, crowding the tough, pale-green fruit

on blankets along the cellar wall. *Devono tutti maturare*
he whispered to me while we worked—I stopped, coaxed one
back into my hand, and held it, its skin beginning
to flood with color, a lantern swelling with light.

The True Story of my Father

There were days when I'd catch him
alone at the kitchen table, lost

inside some regret, his head
cradled in his hands like the part

of his life that was over, that had
stopped some time ago. A cigarette
smoldered beside him, its smoke
rising from the ashtray like a long

held breath, slowly released.
I would like to say that my mother
went to him then, leaned over to
whisper his name in his ear,

and he jerked up, a little startled,
staring around the room in unrecognition,
having been called back too quickly
into his life, and looked up

at my mother who smiled, running
her long fingers through his hair,
slipping them into its dark glistening.
I would like this, finally, to be

a story of love. But the truth is
my father was an unhappy man,
his head was heavy, and sometimes
he rested it in his hands.

Caserta, Italy — 1945

My uncle and aunt pose in front
of their first automobile. They look tired.

Their heads tilt slightly down, away
from the sun, as though having

just climbed out of some dim cellar
where all night, huddled, they listened

to heavy rain surge across the roof.
(*The war swept through our streets*

like a storm he would later say.)
Behind them, along the street, repairs

are already underway, two men
on a roof lift their flat hammers

in a simultaneous strike, their arms raised
as if in casual salute. Some falling bricks

have just scattered a flock of sparrows
that rise to fruit the devastated trees.

Everything, it seems, is poised and ready
for these two, who smile, a little in love

with their own image, two travellers
on a deck, at night, in fog, a few

possessions stuffed in their pockets.
They have no idea of what they will

have to endure; how, in her last winter,
she will fight to stay awake, holding on

to each day, watching snow dampen
the glass on the hospital window;

or how, in the spring, he will stand
at her grave, surrounded by the green release

of leaves, the traffic nosing through wet streets.
They want their lives to shine, the way

the car behind them shines, a raw gleam
of sunlight across its dark chrome hood.

Look, they seem to be saying, the war
is over. We survive. We have this car.

The Inheritance

A large freezer in the cellar
filled with food my aunt
left cooling for years: walnuts
with chipped shells, bruised

bananas, cookies nibbled
by guests, half-eaten apples
that had browned, pasta
left on plates—everything

frozen until some future date
when it could all be rescued.
During dinners, my uncle
always joked that one day

my aunt might mistakenly
refrigerate *him*; with all of us
watching he'd stiffen
into a crouch, open his mouth

on an arrested scream,
and raise his hands with fingers
painfully curled from
clawing at the fridge door.

My aunt giggled whenever he
performed this, her face blooming
bright red as she held back
the laughter. The truth was

my aunt took care of my uncle
completely, managing his needs
with a devotion that anticipated
and provided for every desire:

camomile tea a half-hour
before bed, a back-rub while
reading Il *Corriere Italiano*,
a basin of warm water

for his aching feet. There was
something about her dedication
that made me think of a once
exuberant passion: not so much

used up as outlived. After we
drove home from her funeral,
my uncle took his place
at the kitchen table, and all

the older women immediately
grew busy, laying out the food
friends and family had brought,
finding the good set of dishes,

acting as though they belonged.
My uncle seemed to scarcely
notice anything, just stared
at his hands, lying limp against

the tabletop, while his immense
self-pity, his need for sympathy
closed around us, a cold airless
space that muffled every sound.

Shannon Stewart

Shannon Stewart is a Vancouver writer, teacher and mother whose poetry has appeared in a number of Canadian journals. She received an MFA in Creative Writing from UBC, where she worked as Poetry Editor for PRISM *International*.

For a Bouquet

My meals always taste better for a bouquet, or a moss-plate, or a pot of fern in the middle of the table. In summer we use fresh flowers. It does not take long to gather a few and put them in a little vase or glass, and it cheers the whole family up to see them.

—COUSIN ANN, THE COMPLETE HOME
(A Victorian book of house-keeping)

Where others have not given
a second thought, you pluck
these ladies whole and shining
from the junk tables of Sunday sales.
The roll of a voluptuous lip, porcelain
bodice of cream, this one rich and cold
in her cobalt coat, that one slightly
mad, her green glass luminous
where an eye pressed close

swims like a startled fish
in a sea of cut stems.
One cupboard diachronous
with the tall, round, plain and pure;
where a hand reaching in
might pull out any family's past,
the dimpled silver gracing Sunday's company,
the miniature in the sick child's room.
How you let them riot now,
in the center of your table,
like hands cupping
what is most dear to them,
cottonwood, lilac, branches of maple,
as if you always knew
love is this exact abundance
of shape and odour and disarray,
where the hairline crack runs
over the water, dark seam of use
cleaving us all.

My Mother and Asparagus

In the spring use freely greens, as beet or turnip greens, dandelions, spinach, very young milk-weed, lamb's quarters, etc. Also eat asparagus freely: it is a nervine.

—AUNT SOPHRONIA, THE COMPLETE HOME

In her green coat, marching up the hill from the supermarket, the bundles of asparagus poking out from the brown paper bags. At home, she rolls off the red elastic and from the quiver of her white hand they spill like arrows across the table. She steams them in the coffee percolator, where they won't get bruised, stands them up gently, the swaying stalks of a forest pale before the storm. Through the thick glass bubble in the lid I see the tips burst into a green that doesn't belong to the kitchen, the dulled pots and counters and the sink full of dishes.

I am allowed to eat them with my fingers, she says it is the only way to eat
asparagus, the delicate spears across my plate, hot and buttery, my tongue
finding the small nubs at the tips.

And later on, in the bathroom where she has just been, the smell of
asparagus pee filling the small room, the musk of something gold and green
and I imagine her there, the bright archer, crouched and ready, her eyes
closed in the odour of it, the bow singing through fern and lily.

Books

I've heard one Victorian lady
arranged her bookshelves
with a grand propriety.
Careful to separate
the male and female authors.
Who knew what might happen
if blind old Milton
was left to stand too long
by the wit of Austen?
What illicit catastrophe,
mingling between the covers
in the dark of night?
I love that woman, whoever
she was, chaste even with
the dry pages of her books,
believing they were capable
of anything, when her back
was turned.

Like when we were kids,
even before we could read,
closing up our picture books,
our thumbs marking the page,
and then throwing them open again,

suddenly, expecting to find
something changed, the young princess
dancing and carrying on,
when she should have been beautiful
and sleeping, the prince ugly,
the monster
someone we recognized.

Anything could happen
inside that book,
when you closed it.

Or when you opened it,
which is how we became friends.
Reading that line of Donne's:
God shall create us all Doctors
In a minute.
Abandoning our study notes
on metaphysical poetry,
getting drunk on wine instead.
Deciding that was the best thing
we'd learned all year.

You told me about the summer
you worked in a secondhand bookstore.
How you loved
the boxes of old novels.
How you took them out
one by one, holding
their wobbly spines,
shaking them gently,
waiting to see
what would fall to the ground.
Ancient flowers, small
crisps of leaves and once,
a seahorse, a gallant little man,

with a brittle chest,
riding the wave of words.
You gave him to me,
saying he was the sort of thing
you'd thought I'd like,
still intact after all those years
of living inside a book.

And you also tell me about the calligraphy
of signatures inside a cover.
How men used initials,
but women scrawled their whole names,
intimately, carefully.
The Bessies, Amelias, and Ediths.
Women not afraid to be left inside
when the cover closed,
and it got dark.

I'm learning
it's also where books open to.
Like my favourite book of poems
I know inside out.
Every time I take it in my hands,
it parts to a poem I love.
But finding the same book
on your shelf, it opens to
different pages, poems
I've never read before,
so that it opens into you,
showing me the places
you've been touched,
your delicate spots
I hadn't known until
the book showed me where.

Renovations

While the son must be taught some business of life, there is one business which should always be taught a daughter—the business of housekeeping, in all its departments.
—AUNT SOPHRONIA, THE COMPLETE HOME

We were on our knees
in the laundry room
tiling the floor.
My father moved beside me
spreading the patches of grout.
I fixed the tiles side by side,
wiping the edges clean.
I don't think
we said much.
It was enough to feel
the roughness of cement
under my hands, to hear
the furnace hissing and clicking
in a rhythm
I had not imagined
that hollow can
of green metal could keep.
And the washer and dryer gleaming
in the pure realm of my mother,
how their cold sides
groaned a little
when our shoulders bumped against them
in our work.
I liked this.
I wanted to be good and careful and quick
and my father must have seen it.
Must have known how hard
I was working to keep up
and it must have pained him,

his small daughter with his own
love and haste and sweat for the job,
knowing she knew the feel
of her palms and knees
on the dank floor, hovering
in the raw chemical smells of renovation,
learning how true and fine
that could be with the radio voices
rolling across the bare room
and the bare light almost warm
on the back of her neck.
It must have pained him because he said
It wouldn't always be like this.
That one day I would turn sixteen
and selfish.
Boy-crazy, is what he said.
Too busy with boys
to help your father at night.
I stooped lower then,
the smell of the grout turning sour
and maybe he regretted
having said what he did
seeing me deny it, saying
No Never I won't
even then as that older girl
broached my side
like a curved bright hook between us.
I pressed the tiles
faster now, in neat rows,
willing them stuck forever,
as the furnace roared up behind us,
its warm breath
filling the rooms above.

Architecture

You have lit a room in me,
my walls taut
as a lamp's wire harp
circling the bare bulb.
Navel pushed out,
small skylight
in the white dome of flesh
risen from the hips
like a city I have seen
built on stilts, the boats
with the people in them
floating beneath.

Circle Jerk

It is this circle jerk thing that gets me,
a ritual of childhood I never had.
I imagine a group of boys on their knees
busily frantic in the front,
clutching their half-grown cocks
and groaning, smiling, doing whatever
they have to do just to get the stuff out.
I'm not making fun, in fact,
I think it's rather grand, boys sharing
like that, I think of their faces, the expression
of grief and relief, the spasm of coming
into the privacy of the boy next to him.
And I try not to think of whatever lies in the middle,
the cookie or cracker, which is probably a myth anyway.
But even this is ripe with religious intent.
The last to come made to eat the wafer shot with seed.

I try and imagine a group of girls sitting
on chairs doing the same thing. Their fingers
twirling under cotton panties, knees
flung wide, rosy nipples rasping against
their undershirts. It just doesn't work
and it's hard to say why. Maybe because a girl
wouldn't want another girl seeing her like that,
her face faltering and twitching and stupidly numb
before such ecstasy. It just wouldn't do. Or maybe
it would if only she had something to aim for,
like a cookie or a page torn from a magazine, but
what then would she aim with, how shoot into the center
claiming the bull's eye with her come?

With girls it wouldn't be a game.
But I wish it could be.
I need all the rituals I can get, so instead
I imagine six of them there, in a circle, legs
spread, their twelve knees holding up
a huge world between them, filled with
the pattern of oceans and ice flows and deserts
their knees encircling the planet
like an equator burning with the same degree of desire.

And the last one to come,
the awkward one the delicate one the one who was so slow
and went through so much pain in getting here,
we'd give her the whole shining globe
and we'd say:
Here, take this.
Swallow this.
It's yours.

Acknowledgements

We would especially like to thank everyone who submitted. You gave us
hours of fascinating reading and reconfirmed in our faith in the originality
and diversity of our country's poetry. If the book had been larger,
many of you would have been included. We'll keep an eye out for your
poems in magazines and books in years to come.

We want to pay tribute to the generosity of the poets who appear here,
and to their publishers, who allowed us to include their work for
such a small fee. The cooperation of many Canadian presses was crucial
to the publication of this book.

Finally, we are grateful to Harbour Publishing, especially Howard
White, who over a bottle of wine one night at our house agreed to
take on this project though he knew it would be a financial headache.
For thirty years he and his wife, Mary, have never swayed from their
commitment to poetry. At the press, it was Marisa Alps whose energy
and diligence kept the whole thing together and on schedule. Although
Marisa's poems are included, she submitted under a pseudonym (the
infamous Ann Wong) and completely fooled us. We're delighted her poems
begin the book.

— LORNA CROZIER AND PATRICK LANE

Credits

Bourne, Lesley-Anne. "Cars and Fast–Food" and "My Mother Turns Fifty" from *The Story of Pears*, Penumbra Press 1991. "Think of Him," "Night Before" and "In the Past" from *Skinny Girls*, Penumbra Press, 1993. Poems published courtesy of Penumbra Press.

Bowling, Tim. "The Last Sockeye," "Young Eagle on a Piling" and "Tides (A Poem to Myself)" from *Low Water Slack*, Nightwood Editions, 1995. Reprinted courtesy of Nightwood Editions.

Connelly, Karen. "From My Father's Hand," "Family Reunions" and "Singing" from *The Small Words in My Body*, © 1990, 1995 by Karen Connelly, published by Gutter Press, 1995. "The Word Is Absurd," "The Ugly Mermaid," "She Returns To The Farm" and "Love has nothing to do with closing your eyes" from *This Brighter Prison: A Book of Journeys*, by Karen Connelly and published by Brick Books, 1993. Poems reprinted courtesy of Gutter Press and Brick Books.

Ito, Sally. "On Translating the Works of Akiko Yosano," "Portrait of Snow Country," "Sansei," "Jews in Old China," "Night in Prospector's Valley" and "Frogs in the Rain Barrel" from *Frogs in the Rain Barrel*, Nightwood Editions, 1995. Reprinted courtesy of Nightwood Editions.

Klar, Barbara. "The Home," "Meadowing," "Former Sestina For Birds And A Girl" and "Planter's Prayer" from *The Night You Called Me a Shadow*, by Barbara Klar, Coteau Books, 1993. Reprinted courtesy of Coteau Books.

Lau, Evelyn. "Nineteen," "Green," "Eight Months Later: His House," "Father," from *Oedipal Dreams*, © 1992, 1994 by Evelyn Lau. Published by Coach House Press and reprinted by permission. "Where Did You Learn," "The Monks' Song," "Adult Entertainment" and "Waking in Toronto" from *In the House of*